A Williamson *Little Hands®* Book

PAPER PLATE CRAFTS

CREATIVE ART FUN FOR 3- to 7-YEAR-OLDS

Laura Check

✤

Illustrations by

Norma Jean Martin-Jourdenais

WILLIAMSON PUBLISHING • CHARLOTTE, VERMONT

Copyright © 2000 by Laura Check

Library of Congress Cataloging-in-Publication Data

Check, Laura, 1958–
    Little Hands paper plate crafts : creative art fun for 3- to 7-year-olds / Laura Check.
        p. cm. — (A Williamson Little Hands book)
    Includes index.
    ISBN 1-885593-43-0 (pbk.)
    1. Paper work—Juvenile literature. 2. Plates (Tableware)—Juvenile literature. [1. Paper work. 2. Handicraft.] I. Title: Paper plate crafts. II. Title. III. Series.

TT870 .C4733 2000
745.54—dc21
                                                                          00-043483

Little Hands® series editor: **Susan Williamson**
Interior design: **Monkey Barrel Design**
Illustrations: **Norma Jean Martin-Jourdenais**
Cover design: **Trezzo-Braren Studio**
Printing: **Capital City Press**

Williamson Publishing Co.
P.O. Box 185
Charlotte, VT 05445
(800) 234-8791

Manufactured in the United States of America

10 9 8 7 6 5 4 3 2

Little Hands®, *Kids Can!*®, *Tales Alive!*®, and *Kaleidoscope Kids*® are registered trademarks of Williamson Publishing.

Good Times™ and *Quick Starts for Kids!*™ are trademarks of Williamson Publishing.

Dedication

To my friend and original paper plate partner, Mary Lucas, and to the teachers at Hanalei Elementary and Menehune School for letting me photograph some of their students' projects.

Acknowledgments

Special thanks to my husband, Tom, and children — Christopher, Windy, and Sonny — whose imaginations and creative energy turned this book into a fun-filled family project!

Contents

Sea Creatures

It's Wild!

(continued on next page)

MiMiC MaSKS

Hats For Play!

seasonal Fun!

ALL ABOUT Me!

Let's Go!

Take a plate;
    then CREATE!
Get your scissors and some glue —
    paints, sequins, feathers, too!

Look at your plate;
    what do you see —
A snake, a caterpillar,
    or a honeybee?

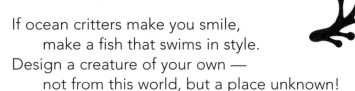

If ocean critters make you smile,
    make a fish that swims in style.
Design a creature of your own —
    not from this world, but a place unknown!

Pretend you're an astronaut
    way out in space,
Or a tiger hiding
    in a secret place.

Make a hat
    for work or play.
Make a new one
    everyday!

Celebrate the seasons
    all through the year,
Create some sunshine
    for people dear!

With paper plates,
    you can express
All the things
    that you like best!

Take a chance,
    try something new;
There's just no limit
    to the things you can do!

FOR PARENTS AND TEACHERS

Through fun, simple crafts, kids learn that artistic possibilities are everywhere; they discover the creativity and inventiveness within themselves. With a paper plate in hand, kids become artists and inventors expressing their interpretation of the world they live in. They are free to experiment and to surprise themselves with the results. It's a miraculous process; all that's required are some paper plates, paints, decorations, and your enthusiasm for their creativity!

Join in!

The crafts for this book are based on my 10 years experience as a preschool teacher (making hundreds of paper-plate crafts!), as well as my years of art play with my own three children. The six different themes invite kids to participate in whatever interests them, at a comfortable skill level. (Check the skill icons and the accompanying clock face on each activity to get an idea of the skill required and time involved.) Kids can pick and choose the crafts at random, using any activity as a jumping-off point for other projects. Let the child lead, following his or her own interests. These activities are risk-free experiences for the child, with no right or wrong outcomes.

Play and experiment!

Although specific instructions are given with each project, always allow the child to make choices and to follow his or her own method of artistic expression. Avoid setting limits and boundaries on kids' creative expression. Invite them to improve on the projects presented, trying different decorations and textures.

For suggestions of ways to stretch kids' imaginations, see the *Imagine That!* and *More Paper Plate Fun!* sections that accompany each project. The *Story Corners* suggest age-appropriate, fun-filled readings that relate to the projects. Beyond the value of read-aloud time, a *Story Corner* also can trigger kids' imaginations to stretch in new directions. Sometimes I read the

story first to help kids see the world in a new way before they begin their crafts. Remember that the experience of creating is far more important than the finished project. The kids know that — just look at their pride in what they are doing!

If you don't have the craft supplies listed, use whatever you have on hand — seeds, dry beans, pasta noodles, colored rice, and buttons all inspire creativity. Save craft sticks, packing materials, old magazines, catalogs, cards, and ribbons. Collect sequins, sparkles, craft feathers, dried flowers and leaves, and colorful pebbles and shells.

Have Fun!

One of the greatest things about using paper plates is their low cost and availability, so don't hesitate to keep handing them out for countless, wonderful masterpieces. Most of all, enjoy this special time you have together, creating art with the children in your life.

Make it Safe!

When using paints, put out just a few colors at a time in small, stable containers with a paintbrush in each color. Have rags ready for painted fingers, and provide an old T-shirt or painting smock for kids to wear over their clothes. With most preschoolers, the more paint the better; however, with paper plates, too much paint will weaken the plates and they won't hold their shape. Try using cut-and-paste pictures or have kids draw with markers and crayons.

An adult must always be present when kids are making art and crafts. Always have children use child safety scissors and a small school stapler. Substitute glue for the staples, if necessary, to make the activity more suitable to very young children. Be ready to assist with (not take over!) the more difficult cutting, stapling, hole punching, and threading, if necessary. (When a child needs help, ask her where she wants you to staple or cut.)

Young artists may still have a tendency to put small objects in their mouths. Any projects requiring paper fasteners, buttons, or other small objects should be closely supervised by an adult. Control the supply of small objects by keeping them in your pocket and distributing as needed.

Sea Creatures

Get ready to discover the magical world in the ocean's depths! Imagine all the colors, shapes, and patterns on the animals that live in and near the ocean. Think about how the ocean makes you feel, look at pictures of real sea creatures and coral reefs — and then create your *own* underwater world. There's no limit to the variety of sea creatures (real and pretend!) that can be brought to life with paper plates!

FaBULoUS FiSH

*Colorful fish
in the sea,
Swimming together
right past me!*

What You Need

2 large paper plates
(or 1 large plate and plate scraps)

Child safety scissors

Stapler

Markers

Tempera paints

Paintbrushes

Glitter

Glue

☆ Here We Go! ☆

1 Cut out the mouth.

2 Staple the cutout piece onto the body for a tail fin.

3 Cut out the top and bottom fins from the second plate. Staple to the body.

4 Decorate with markers, paints, and glitter.

◎ More Paper Plate Fun! ◎

Story Corner: For some more fishy fun, take a look at *The Rainbow Fish* by Marcus Pfister and *Louis the Fish* by Arthur Yorlinks.

SCALLOP SURPRISE

Beautiful shell on the sand, Its yellows and oranges brighten our land!

Imagine That!

Our skeletons are inside our bodies, but a scallop wears its skeleton on the outside! The curved lines on the shell tell how old it is. How old will your scallop be?

back

fold and staple

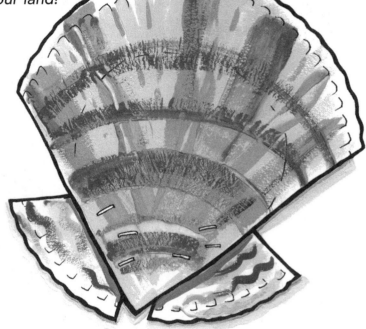

What You Need ✏️

2 large paper plates (or 1 large plate and plate scraps)

Stapler

Child safety scissors

Tempera paints

Paintbrushes

☆ Here We Go! ☆

1 Fold the sides of the plate under to form a point. Staple.

2 Cut out two triangle pieces from the scraps. Staple to the point.

3 Decorate with paints.

◎ More Paper Plate Fun! ◎

Start a Collection: Collect *empty* shells at the beach. Glue them together to make funny animals, decorate boxes, or create a display. No shells around? Start a collection of buttons or rocks.

SWIFT SEA TURTLE

*Up to the surface
for a breath of air,
The swift sea turtle
doesn't have a care!*

1 Cut out the head, tail, and feet from one plate.

2 Staple to the other plate.

3 Decorate with markers and glitter. Glue on buttons.

What You Need ✏

Child safety scissors

2 large paper plates

Stapler

Markers

Glue

Glitter

Buttons

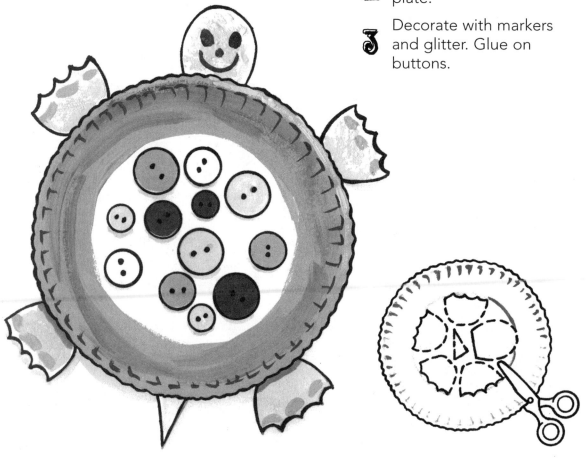

◎ More Paper Plate Fun! ◎

Art Play: Instead of using buttons, make a pattern on the shell using bottle caps, erasers, or a sliced radish dipped in paints.

☆ Here We Go! ☆

1 Cut the rims from the plates into at least three sections, cutting one wider rim for the head with its back fin.

2 Cut out the mouth on the head piece.

3 Staple the rims in opposite directions to make the curving body.

4 Decorate with paints and glitter.

Imagine That!

What snake-like fish can grow as long as a car? Yes, eels! They have beautiful colors and interesting designs — and some even glow in the dark! How long are you going to make your curving eel, and what "electrifying" colors will you choose?

◎ More Paper Plate Fun! ◎

Art Play: Make a beautiful design on your eel using paints but no paintbrush! Just dab on some colors with a sponge to get a one-of-a-kind pattern! Add glitter to catch the light as your eel goes slithering by.

Try sponge-painting your eel!

creative crab

*The busy crab
runs across the sand;
You better watch out
or it'll tickle your hand!*

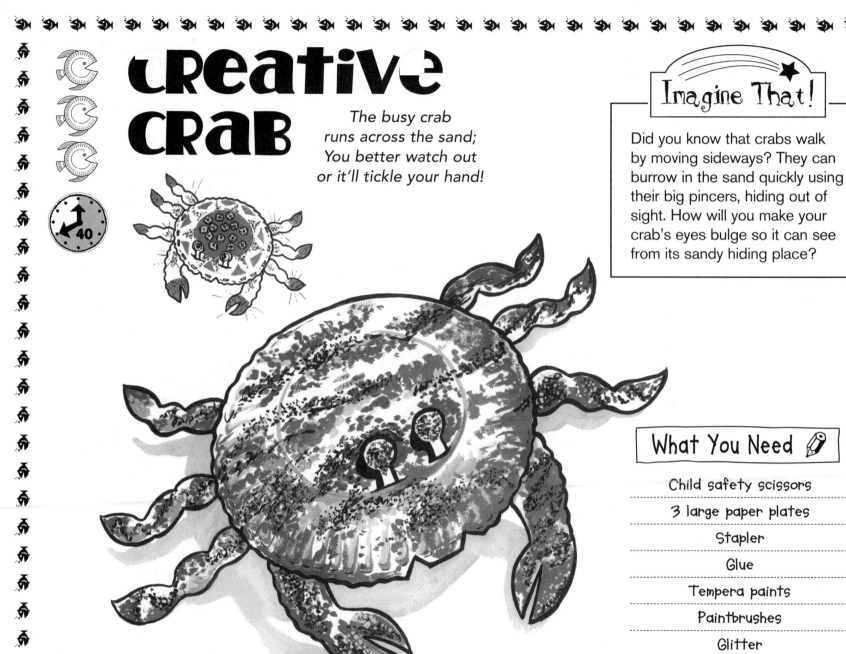

Imagine That!

Did you know that crabs walk by moving sideways? They can burrow in the sand quickly using their big pincers, hiding out of sight. How will you make your crab's eyes bulge so it can see from its sandy hiding place?

What You Need ✏

Child safety scissors

3 large paper plates

Stapler

Glue

Tempera paints

Paintbrushes

Glitter

☆ Here We Go! ☆

1 Cut out six crab legs, a pair of pincers, and two eyes from one plate.

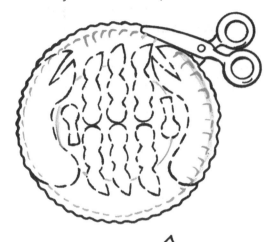

2 Staple the legs and pincers to the second plate.

3 Glue or staple the third plate on top.

4 Cut out small triangles for the crab's mouth.

insert eyes through slits and fold back →

◎ More Paper Plate Fun! ◎

Art Play: Here are three ways to decorate your crab:

(1) **Use a sponge** dipped in paint to get a unique *camouflage* design (camouflage means the crab blends in with its surroundings).

(2) **Add pizzazz** to your crab shell with glitter or sequins.

(3) **Cut and paste designs** from construction paper or magazines for a textured look.

5 Make slits in the top plate; insert eyes so that they sit up (bulging).

6 Decorate with paints and glitter.

JiGGLY JeLLYFiSH

*It looks like a bubble
floating in the sea,
With long stringy tentacles —
what could it be?*

What You Need

2 large heavy-duty paper plates

Child safety scissors

Stapler

Tempera paints

Paintbrushes

Pencil

Yarn

Glue

Glitter

Imagine That!

If you've ever seen a jellyfish washed up on a beach, you know how it got its name — it looks like a big blob of jelly! Now, how can you make a soft jellyfish out of a stiff paper plate? Hmmm — that will take some imagination!

AWESOME OCTOPUS

*Eight long arms,
two little eyes,
A big soft body —
what a slippery surprise!*

☆ Here We Go! ☆

1 Cut out the body shape.

2 Paint; decorate with glitter.

3 Tape eight streamers to the bottom of the plate for arms.

4 Make googly eyes however you want!

What You Need ✐

Child safety scissors

Large paper plate

Tempera paints

Paintbrushes

Glue and Glitter

Tape

Streamers

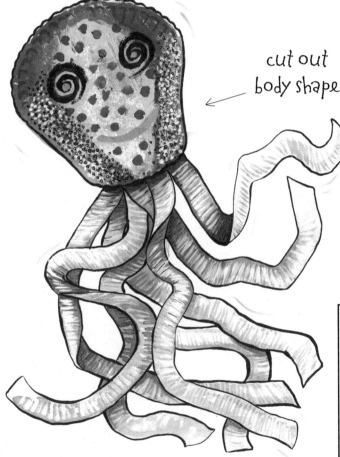

cut out
body shape

More Paper Plate Fun! ◎

Story Corner: For more ocean fun, listen to *Commotion in the Ocean* by Giles Andreae.

Imagine That! ★

We made our octopus's long, long *tentacles* (arms) out of crepe paper streamers. What else could you use to make those eight, l-o-n-g arms? What are you going to use for the big googly eyes?

LURKIN' URCHIN

With red and purple spines sticking up, It looks like a prickly upside down cup!

40

What You Need

Child safety scissors

Large heavy-duty paper plate

Stapler

Newspaper

Glue

Large regular paper plate

Tempera paints

Paintbrushes

Glitter

☆ Here We Go! ☆

1 Cut out four triangles from the heavy-duty plate as shown.

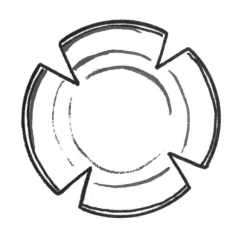

Imagine That!

What a funny-looking creature! A sea urchin's spines protect it as it crawls along the sea floor feeding on plants and animals. How will you make protective spines for your paper-plate sea urchin? (We used rolled–up paper. What ideas do you have?)

2 Overlap and staple the cut-out plate to form the body.

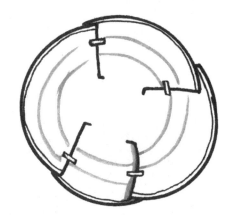

3 Roll up scraps of newspaper for spines.

4 Poke holes through the body. Push the spines through. Glue each spine to hold it in place.

5 Trim the rim of the other plate to fit under the body. Glue in place.

6 Paint and decorate your urchin.

◎ More Paper Plate Fun! ◎

Story Corner: Check out some other amazing sea life in *Totally Amazing Sea Creatures* by Iqbal Hussain.

StinGRaY!

He flaps his body,
just like wings;
But watch where you step
'cause he just might sting!

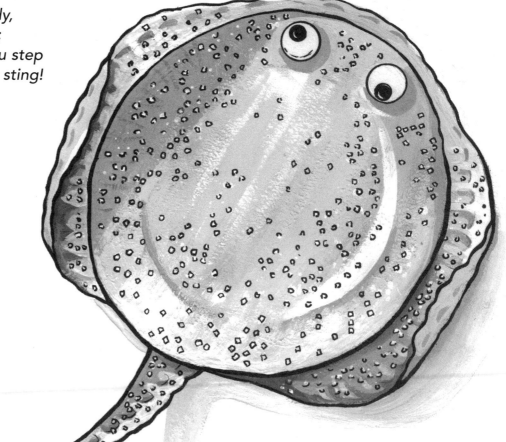

What You Need 🖉

Child safety scissors

2 large paper plates

Glue

Cotton balls
or crumpled newspaper

Stapler

Tempera paints

Paintbrushes

Glitter

Wiggly eyes

◎ More Paper Plate Fun! ◎

Pretend Play: All rays swim by flapping
their bodies. Can you flap your arms like
a ray? Make believe you're swimming fast
through the water, stingray fashion!

bottom plate

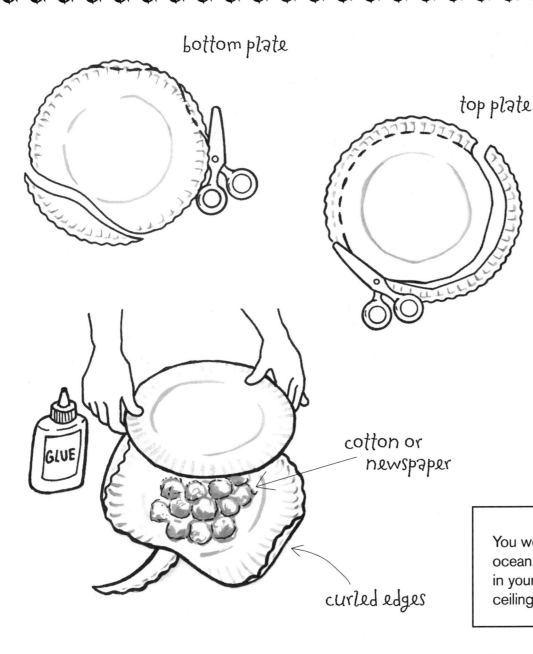

top plate

cotton or newspaper

GLUE

curled edges

1 Trim the bottom plate in a ray shape. Curl the rays up.

2 Trim off $\frac{1}{2}$" (1 cm) around the rim of the top plate.

3 Glue cotton or newspaper onto the top of the bottom plate. Glue the trimmed top plate over the bottom plate.

4 Cut out a tail from the trimmings. Staple to the bottom plate.

5 Paint. Add glitter and wiggly eyes.

Imagine That!

You wouldn't want to meet a stringray out in the ocean, but this paper-plate stingray can live right in your room! Add a string and hang it from your ceiling for an "undersea" scene at home!

STaRRY StaRFiSH

⏱ 20

The friendly starfish
slowly creeps by,
Coming your way
just to say, "Hi!"

Stuff for fullness!

Imagine That!

Most starfish have five arms, but some
have as many as 25, and the giant
starfish can have 50 arms — wow! You
know what is even more amazing? If a
starfish loses an arm, it grows a new
one. How many arms do you want your
starfish to have?

☆ **Here We Go!** ☆

What You Need

Child safety scissors

2 large paper plates

Cotton balls or newspaper

Stapler

Tempera paints

Paintbrushes

Sequins or stars

1 Cut both plates at the
same time in a starfish
shape.

2 Stuff cotton balls or
crumpled newspaper
between the plates.

3 Staple edges together.

4 Paint and decorate
with sequins and stars.

〇 More Paper Plate Fun! 〇

Story Corner: For a glimpse
of other interesting ocean
shapes, look at *Sea Shapes*
by Suse MacDonald.

IT'S WILD!

What can you find on a trek through the tall grass, way up in trees, or out in the hot desert? A whole lot of interesting creatures, that's what! In the wild, there are flying, hopping, slithering animals of every size, shape, and color! Mix the brightest colors and use your paper plates to create designs only you can imagine. Go ahead, be wild!

BaBY BiRD

*Baby bird
with feathers so light,
Flies up in the sky
just like a kite!*

What You Need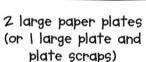

2 large paper plates
(or 1 large plate and
plate scraps)

Child safety scissors

Tape

Stapler

Tempera paints

Paintbrushes or sponges

Glue

Button

◎ More Paper Plate Fun! ◎

Story Corner: Read *Are You My Mother?* by P.D. Eastman and *I Bought a Baby Chicken* by Kelly Milner Halls.

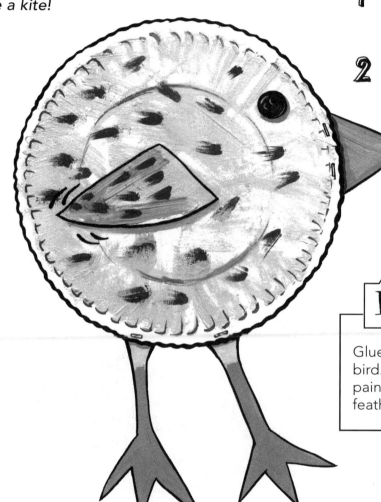

1 Cut feet, beak, and wing from the plate scraps. Tape or staple onto the full-sized plate.

2 Paint with a sponge or brush. Glue on a button eye.

Imagine That!

Glue craft feathers onto your bird. Then, try sponging paints over them for another feathery look.

LUCKY LADYBUG

20

No cutting needed!

Lucky ladybug,
don't fly away!
Please stay and visit —
so we can play!

What You Need

Large heavy-duty paper plate

Red and black tempera paints

Paintbrushes

Glue

Felt or pom-poms

Pipe cleaners

Beads

Imagine That!

Attach a strip (with tape or glue) on the underside of the plate so you can slide your hand in and fly your ladybug.

☆ Here We Go! ☆

1 Paint the back of the plate red.

2 When dry, outline the wings and face with black paint.

3 Glue on felt pieces or use pom-poms for your ladybug's spots and eyes.

4 Poke two holes in the head for antennae. Weave pipe cleaners through, twist, and thread a bead on each end.

More Paper Plate Fun!

Story Corner: Read *The Grouchy Ladybug* by Eric Carle.

Colorful Caterpillar

*Eating and growing
as it crawls along,
It won't be a caterpillar
for very long!*

30

bend pipe cleaners
from hole to hole

What You Need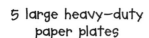

5 large heavy-duty
paper plates

Tempera paints

Paintbrushes

Stapler

Child safety scissors

Pipe cleaners

☆ Here We Go! ☆

1 Paint a design on the back of each plate.

2 Staple the plates together.

3 Cut pipe cleaners.

4 Poke two holes in one side of each plate. Weave the pipe cleaners through for feet. On the first plate, add pipe-cleaner antennae. Curl up a pipe cleaner for an eye.

Imagine That!

After eating and growing and eating and growing some more, a caterpillar spins a cocoon (called a *chrysalis*). Inside, it's transformed into a beautiful butterfly or moth! Will you make a tiny baby caterpillar (using two plates) or a great big caterpillar (five plates) that's ready to spin a cocoon? What colorful design will your caterpillar wear?

◎ More Paper Plate Fun! ◎

Art Play: Here are other ways to decorate your caterpillar: (1) Glue on buttons. (2) Use yarn for bright stripes. Fantastic!

Nature Play: Carefully collect caterpillars from milkweed plants and care for them in a cage with plenty of fresh milkweed leaves. Observe up close how the caterpillars turn into beautiful monarch butterflies. Then, watch them fly away free! Read all about monarchs in *Monarch Magic!* by Lynn M. Rosenblatt.

Story Corner: Read *The Very Hungry Caterpillar* by Eric Carle. Then, paint some plates for the orange, apple, and other foods with little holes eaten through them, and act out the story.

BEAUTIFUL BUTTERFLY

*Stretching its wings,
it flies up high,
Beautiful colors
fill the sky!*

What You Need ✏

2 large paper plates

Tempera paints

Paintbrushes

Child safety scissors

Stapler

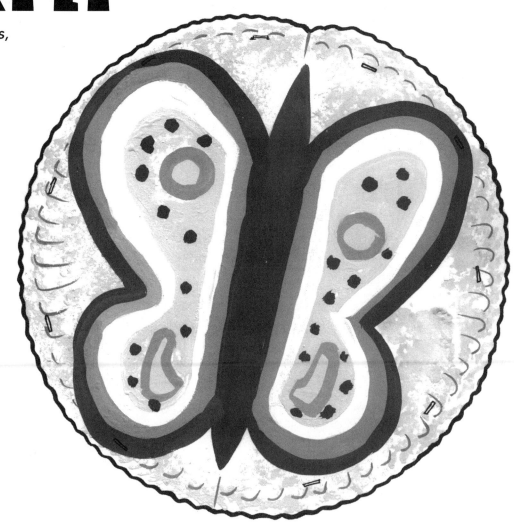

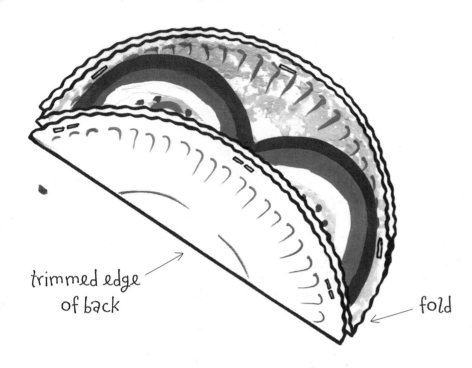

trimmed edge of back

fold

Butterflies look so delicate and light, flitting from flower to flower in search of nectar. Some have bold markings to scare away birds; others blend in with the flowers. All of them are beautiful. What colors and designs will you use?

☆ Here We Go! ☆

1 Paint a butterfly on one plate.

2 Cut the second plate in half. Trim $\frac{1}{2}$" (1 cm) off of each half.

3 Staple each half to the back of the butterfly plate.

4 Slip your hands in the back and make your butterfly fly high!

⟳ More Paper Plate Fun! ⟳

Art Play: Cut out a butterfly shape from a paper plate. Fold in half. Squeeze a few blobs of tempera paint on *one* side. Fold and press together. Now, open your butterfly for a mirror-image wingspan.

Pretend Play: Make believe you are a butterfly, with arms spread apart. Hold a scarf from hand to hand and flutter and fly. Are you heading off on a long-distance trip or just looking for some lunch?

sweet HONEYBEE

*The yellow and black
honeybee
Buzzes in flowers
right next to me!*

35

What You Need ✏

2 large paper plates

Child safety scissors

Yellow and black tempera paints

Paintbrushes

Stapler

---

2 paper fasteners

Pipe cleaners

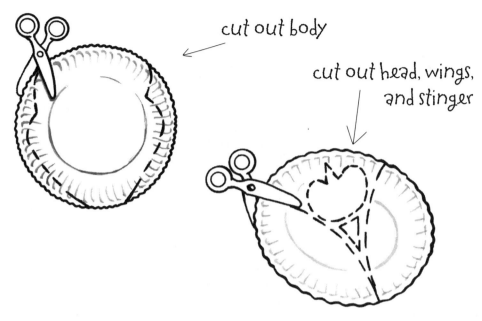

cut out body

cut out head, wings, and stinger

☆ **Here We Go!** ☆

1 Trim the first plate to form the bee's body. Paint.

2 Cut out the head, stinger, and wings from the second plate. Paint.

3 Staple the head and stinger to the body. Attach wings with paper fasteners.

4 Cut pipe cleaners into 2" (5 cm) pieces.

5 Poke six holes in the body and insert pipe-cleaner legs. Poke two holes in the head and insert pipe-cleaner antennae!

☺ More Paper Plate Fun! ☺

Art Play: Cut some felt stripes and glue on for a fuzzier bee, or dip yarn in paint and lay on wings for a great vein design! Attach a hand grip (with tape or glue) on your bee's belly and help him fly!

Story Corner: Read all about bees in *The Magic School Bus: Inside a Beehive* by Joanna Cole and Bruce Degen and *Buzzy the Bumblebee* by Denise Brennan-Nelson.

Imagine That!

Bees do a special dance to tell each other where yummy food is! What dance will you and your honeybee do together?

FRIENDLY SPIDER

20

No cutting needed!

The patient spider doesn't have much to say. It sits and waits quietly for a bug to come its way!

What You Need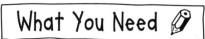

Large heavy-duty paper plate

Tempera paints

Paintbrushes

Hole punch

4 pipe cleaners

Stapler

Ribbon or string

☆ Here We Go! ☆

1 Paint the plate (don't forget the spider's smile!).

2 Punch four pairs of holes in the rim. Wrap a pipe cleaner through two holes, twisting it together in the back. Staple to hold; then, bend the pipe cleaners toward the front. Repeat for the other legs.

3 Punch two holes in the top of your spider. Tie a ribbon through to hang.

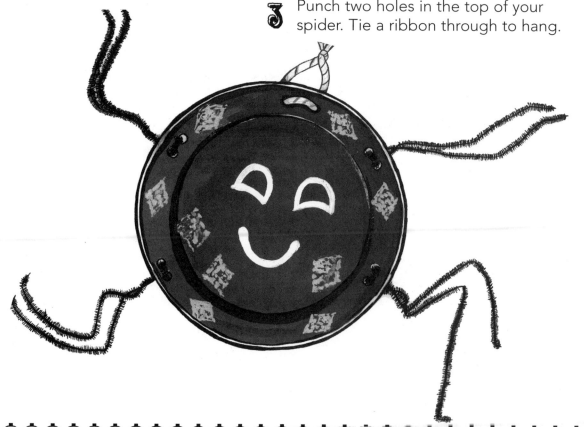

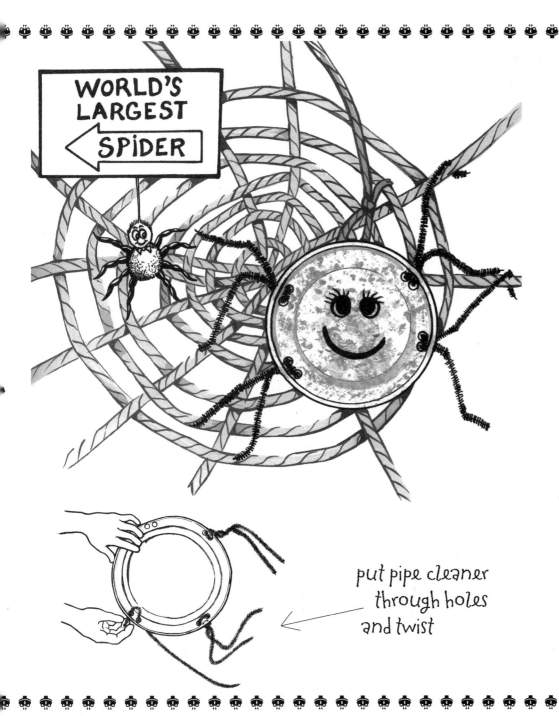

WORLD'S LARGEST SPIDER

put pipe cleaner through holes and twist

Imagine That!

Coming across a spider hanging down from its web can be a little startling — unless you make that spider out of paper plates! What type of spider do you imagine with your paper plate? Where will you hang your friendly spider pal?

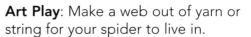

More Paper Plate Fun!

Art Play: Make a web out of yarn or string for your spider to live in.

Just for Fun: Go outside and see if you can spot some real spiders. What type of web do you see? Please don't disturb it!

Story Corner: Read the old favorite *The Eensy-Weensy Spider* by Mary Ann Hoberman. Then, sing and do the hand motions at the same time!

SLITHERING Snake

Snakes softly slither
from side to side,
Searching for
a place to hide!

1 Cut plate into a coil shape.

2 Shape the head.

3 Cut a forked tongue from the plate scraps. Glue it onto the mouth.

4 Paint!

What You Need ✏️

Large paper plate

Child safety scissors

Glue

Tempera paints

Paintbrushes

cut out tongue
from scraps

Imagine That!

Some people think a snake's skin looks slimy and smooth, but actually its skin is scaly and dry. Glue a design of cut-felt pieces or ripped magazine pictures onto your snake's body. Add yarn for stripes or sequins for spots!

🌀 **More Paper Plate Fun!** 🌀

Story Corner: Snake lovers will like *Hide and Snake* by Keith Baker and *Small Green Snake* by Libba Moore Gray.

SLow Snail

*Slowly but surely
the snail finds his way
Across the yard —
it takes him all day!*

☆ Here We Go! ☆

1 Cut out a tail, head, and antennae from one plate. Staple to the other plate.

2 Paint and decorate.

What You Need ✏

Child safety scissors
----
2 large paper plates

Stapler

Tempera paints

Paintbrushes

Markers

Glue and glitter

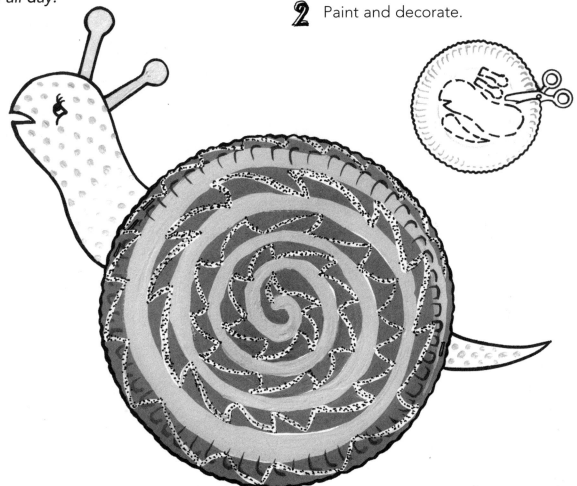

⊚ More Paper Plate Fun! ⊚

Art Play: Paint a bright, wild spiral design on your snail's shell. Add sequins, jewels, glitter, and buttons. Use brightly colored pipe cleaners for antennae.

TOM TURKEY

*Tom Turkey
is a big, big bird
With the loudest gobble
you ever have heard!*

What You Need ✏️

Large paper plate

Tempera paints

Paintbrushes

Child safety scissors

Poster board

Old magazines

Construction paper

Stapler

Glue

☆ Here We Go! ☆

1 Paint the plate for the turkey's body.

2 Cut out a head and six feathers from poster board. Paint the head; cut out colorful pictures from magazines and glue to the feathers. Staple the head and feathers to the plate.

3 Cut out feet and a hat from construction paper. Glue in place.

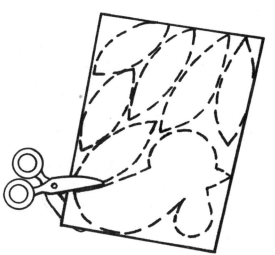

glue pictures from magazines to the feathers

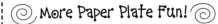

Imagine That!

Boy turkeys are called "gobblers" or "Toms." Girl turkeys are "hens," and baby turkeys are "poults." What a lot of names! Which one will you make — a poult with a bonnet or cap, a Tom with a big, black top hat, or a hen with a fancy feathered hat?

◎ More Paper Plate Fun! ◎

Art Play: Add a bow tie or glasses to your turkey. Glue on buttons.

Story Corner: Listen to the story *A Turkey for Thanksgiving* by Eve Bunting.

BIG-MOUTH FROG

 25

Cool and quiet,
the big green frog
Sits and hides
under a big brown log!

What You Need

2 large paper plates

Child safety scissors

Stapler

2 egg-carton sections

Glue

Tempera paints

Paintbrushes

Ribbit!

☆ Here We Go! ☆

1 Fold one plate in half.

2 Trim $\frac{1}{2}$" (1 cm) from the second plate; then, cut plate in half.

3 Staple each trimmed half to the back of the folded plate.

4 Glue two upside-down egg sections on top for googly eyes.

5 Paint! Add a big felt tongue!

Imagine That!

Frogs make a great big sound: *Ribbit!* What pretend kind of voice will your paper-plate frog have? Will your frog be bright and flashy or *camouflaged* so it's harder to spot?

trimmed edges

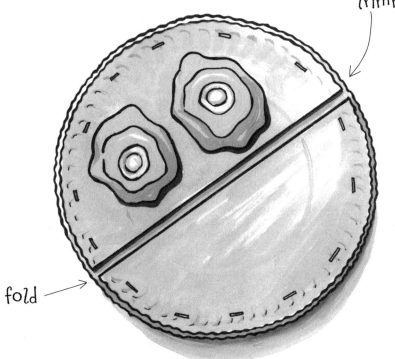

fold

☺ More Paper Plate Fun! ☺

Just for Fun: Play leapfrog together, each player hopping over the ones in front.

Story Corner: For some "hoppy" books, read *The Magic School Bus Hops Home: A Book About Animal Habitats* by Joanna Cole and Bruce Degen or *Tuesday* by David Wiesner.

TEXTURED TORTOISE

*The tortoise's shell
is a special place;
Safe and snug,
it's a cozy space!*

35

Imagine That!

Your tortoise's shell can have whatever design you like! We suggest using cut sponge shapes, doilies, or even your own thumbprints for an interesting *pattern*.

What You Need ✏️

Large heavy-duty paper plate
- -
Child safety scissors
- -
Stapler
- -
Tempera paints
- -
Sponge
- -
Doily
- -
5 egg-carton sections
- -
Glue
- -
Markers

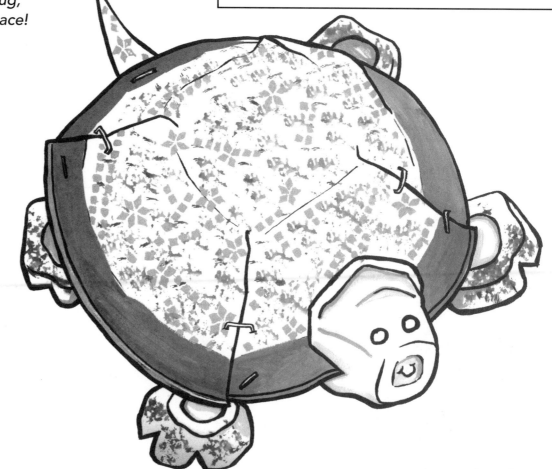

☆ **Here We Go!** ☆

1 Cut out four triangles from the plate as shown.

2 Overlap and staple the plate to form a shell.

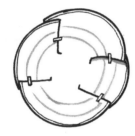

3 Paint the shell with a sponge, pressing over a doily for an interesting pattern.

4 Trim four egg-carton sections; glue on for feet.

trim feet

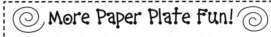

◎ More Paper Plate Fun! ◎

Pretend Play: What kind of home would you like to carry on your back? Make yourself a turtle shell out of a cardboard box and curl up inside! Then, act out the famous fable *The Tortoise and the Hare.*

Story Corner: For more tortoise reads, try *The Foolish Tortoise* by Richard Buckley and Eric Carle and *The Turtle and the Moon* by Charles Turner.

5 Cut slits in one egg-carton section for your tortoise's head. Glue in place.

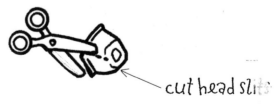

cut head slits

6 Decorate with markers.

WiLD, WiLD AniMaL!

Strange and unusual animals roam Through forests and jungles, they're coming home!

What You Need ✏

Large paper plate

Pencil

Child safety scissors

Stapler

Glue

Markers or tempera paints and paintbrushes

☆ Here We Go! ☆

1 Fold the plate in half. (The fold is your animal's back.)

2 Draw the head, feet, and tail. Cut along the line around the feet, head, and tail. Leave the top folded.

3 Staple or glue on horns, tusks, spikes, or other details. Paint or color with markers on both sides.

4 Open the plate slightly and stand your creature up!

this is the fold

Imagine That!

If you could make up your own animal, what would it be? The body of a hippo with a neck like a giraffe and a trunk like an elephant? Have fun creating the wildest wild creature you can imagine!

◎ More Paper Plate Fun! ◎

Art Play: Gather some grasses, seeds, and fallen bark to create a jungle or forest for your animal to live in!

Pretend Play: See how many different wild animal sounds you can make! Which sound best matches your animal creation?

Story Corner: Read *No Such Things* by Bill Peet.

DiNoSaUR FUN!

*Spikes and horns,
skin like leather;
Did the dinosaurs disappear
due to strange weather?*

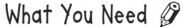

What You Need

Large heavy-duty paper plate

Large regular paper plate

Child safety scissors

Stapler

Glue

Tempera paints

Paintbrushes

☆ Here We Go! ☆

1 Fold the heavy-duty plate as shown to form the body.

2 Cut out the dino's neck and head, and tail from the rim of the regular plate. Staple to the body. Then, staple top of body together.

3 From the regular plate scraps, cut out two rectangles for legs. Fold in thirds and glue in place.

4 Paint your dino. Dino-mite!

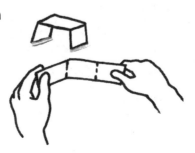

Imagine That!

Dinosaurs roamed the earth 65 million years ago, but they're still tops on our "favorite animals" list. And because no one has seen a living dinosaur, we don't know for sure what colors they were. So, let your imagination take off! Create your own "dino colors" as you discover a new kind of dinosaur with your paper plates!

◎ More Paper Plate Fun! ◎

Art Play: Fold regular plates in half and cut out trees and bushes to make your own dinosaur land.

Story Corner: Discover more dinosaurs in *Dinosaurs Forever* by William Wise and *Dinosaurs Roar!* by Paul and Henrietta Stickland. Learn about dinosaurs in *The Kids' Natural History Book* by Judy Press.

MiMiC MasKS

Do you like to play make-believe? There are so many places you can visit and animals you can become — just by putting on a mask! Become a bunny in a burrow or a wise old owl in a tree, a playful puppy, or a clown in the circus! It's exciting to be something new, especially when it's just pretend. And remember, behind the mask it's really *you*!

Five Quick Animal Masks

*A bunny, a cat,
a pig, bear, or mouse —
What will you be
playing in your house?*

Imagine That!

What type of animal mask do you want to make today? Here are five to get you started. Each one starts out with a heavy-duty paper plate and scraps from a regular paper plate. *You* decide what the critter will be, what type of eyes, nose, mouth, and ears it will have, and what color or texture it will be. Experiment with paints, felt, fake fur, and pipe cleaners to add different features. Make your mask as real or imaginary as you want!

What You Need ✏️

(MAKES ONE MASK)

Large heavy-duty paper plate

Large regular paper plate
or plate scraps

Child safety scissors

Stapler

Glue

Chopstick

Heavy-duty tape

FOR FACE DETAILS:

Egg-carton section

Fabric paint

Felt or quilt batting

Pipe cleaners

Pom-pom

Small paper cup

Tempera paints and
paintbrushes

☆ Here We Go! ☆

1. Poke or cut out eye holes in the plate.

2. Cut ears out of the plate scraps. Staple in place.

3. Paint your mask and glue on or insert face details.

4. Insert the chopstick into the bottom rim of the plate for a holder. Glue and tape it to the back.

MEEK MOUSE

Make round ears

Add cone nose with pom-pom

Add pipe-cleaner whiskers (poked through nose)

Outline ears and eyes with paints; draw on gnawing teeth

PINK PIG

Poke small, round eyes

Bend tips of triangle ears forward

Add egg-carton snout

Paint face and mouth

FUNNY BUNNY

Cut out almond-shaped eyes

Use felt or quilt batting for fur

Add fabric paint details

CURIOUS CAT

Cut out almond-shaped eyes

Paint textured fur

Paint nose, mouth, and eyelashes

Add pipe-cleaner whiskers (poked through plate)

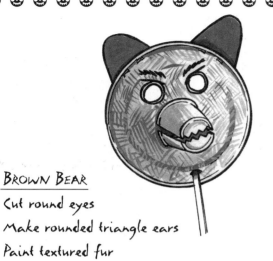

BROWN BEAR

Cut round eyes

Make rounded triangle ears

Paint textured fur

Cut a small paper cup for jaw and teeth

Outline eyes and eyebrows

More Paper Plate Fun!

Art Play: Mix paints to get unusual colors for your critters. Dress up the masks with a bow tie, bows, or ribbons. Add felt stripes, spots, craft fur, or pom-pom noses. Create different characters with varied eye shapes, different-size teeth, and different caps and hats!

Pretend Play: Read a famous tale such as *The Three Little Pigs* and act it out, using your masks!

Story Corner:

Otis by Janie Bynum
Nothing by Mick Inkpen
Frederick by Leo Lionni
Lunch by Denise Fleming

The Bouncy Baby Bunny by Joan Bowden
Mama Cat Has Three Kittens by Denise Fleming
Make a Wish, Honey Bear! by Marcus Pfister

Make It Special!

Textured fur: Run an old comb through a coat of thick paint that's slightly dried.

painted plate

Mouse's cone nose: Cut a triangle about 2" (5 cm) tall from scraps. Staple or glue it into a cone shape for the nose; then, glue it in place.

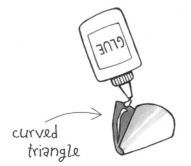

curved triangle

Funny Bunny's furry face: Glue on a piece of felt or quilt batting, covering the paper plate. Cut out the eye holes and trim the material to fit the face. Squeeze on fabric-paint details. (Cover ears with felt or quilt batting, too!)

batting

Brown Bear's paper cup nose with teeth: Cut the paper cup in half, long-wise. Cut teeth in the bottom of each half. Glue the mouth and teeth onto the face.

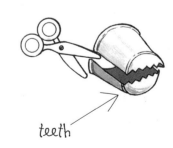

teeth

MARDI GRAS!

20

*Bold and bright,
feathers, too;
Create a mask
just right for you!*

back →

What You Need

Child safety scissors

Large paper plate

Pencil

Tempera paints

Paintbrushes

Glitter

Craft feathers

Glue

Elastic

Stapler

☆ Here We Go! ☆

1 Cut the paper plate to fit over your mouth and nose.

2 Draw and cut out the eye holes.

3 Decorate with paint and glitter. Glue on the feathers.

4 Knot the ends of the elastic; staple them to the back of the mask.

Imagine That!

Mardi Gras, or "Fat Tuesday," is a French carnival held every spring. It's a time for people to dress up in silly costumes and wild masks! How do you want your mask to look — bright and wild, far out, or mysterious? Can you express a *feeling* by using a certain color or by *shaping the eyes* in an unusual way? Make different masks for different looks and moods!

◎ More Paper Plate Fun! ◎

Pretend Play: Have a masquerade party or parade with your friends!

Story Corner: Read *Carl's Masquerade* by Alexandra Day and *Celie and the Harvest Fiddler* by Vanessa and Valerie Flournoy.

PLAYFUL PUPPY

Playful puppy loves to run. Chasing friends is so much fun!

1 Cut out eye holes in one plate.

2 Cut out floppy ears from the second plate.

3 Paint the puppy's ears and face.

4 Attach one ear to each side of the head with paper fasteners.

5 Poke the chopstick into the bottom rim of the plate. Glue and tape to hold in back.

What You Need

2 large heavy-duty plates

Child safety scissors

Tempera paints

Paintbrushes

2 paper fasteners

Chopstick

Glue

Heavy-duty tape

Imagine That!

Puppies are so clumsy and roly-poly — they're always ready to play. And they especially like to tumble with kids like you! Imagine your favorite dog friend as a puppy, and create a mask playmate for him. This mask's ears even move up and down!

back

More Paper Plate Fun!

Art Play: Add some spots to your puppy and a big red tongue! Or, glue on felt, pillow stuffing, or cotton balls for a soft, furry puppy.

Story Corner: Read about two very famous puppies in *Hello, Biscuit!* by Alyssa Satin Capucilli and *Spot Sleeps Over* by Eric Hill.

BRave Lion

*The brave lion
is so very proud.
To let you know,
he roars so loud!*

Imagine That!

The lion is the only wild cat with a mane. Amazing! Think about ways to make your lion's mane look full and fluffy, fit for the king of beasts!

What You Need ✏

Large paper plate

Child safety scissors

Glue

Orange, yellow, and brown felt

Fabric paints

Elastic

Stapler

☆ Here We Go! ☆

1 Cut the paper plate to fit over your mouth and nose. Trim the sides.

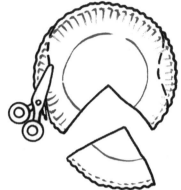

2 Glue the felt to cover the plate. Cut out the eye holes.

3 Cut out and glue on felt shapes for the mane.

4 Paint on the nose and whiskers. Outline the eyes.

5 Knot the ends of the elastic. Staple them to the back of the mask.

back of mask →

◎ **More Paper Plate Fun!** ◎

Art Play: Add yarn strands to your mane. Now, try on the mask and practice roaring like a lion!

Story Corner: For some roaring fun, read *The Lion Who Wanted to Love* by Giles Andreae and David Wojtowycz.

SiLLY CLOWn

*Polka-dotted pants,
big floppy shoes,
Some clowns have happy faces,
and some sing the blues!*

◎ More Paper Plate Fun! ◎

Story Corner: For more circus fun, read *Circus* by Lois Ehlert and *Emeline at the Circus* by Marjorie Priceman.

What You Need

Large paper plate
- - - - - - - - - - - - - - - -
Child safety scissors
- - - - - - - - - - - - - - - -
Tempera paints
- - - - - - - - - - - - - - - -
Paintbrushes
- - - - - - - - - - - - - - - -
Glue
- - - - - - - - - - - - - - - -
Decorations of your choice
- - - - - - - - - - - - - - - -
Stapler
- - - - - - - - - - - - - - - -
Elastic

☆ Here We Go! ☆

1 Cut out eye holes and a mouth from the paper plate in whatever shapes you like.

2 Paint different colors around the eyes and mouth (don't forget a nose and cheeks!).

3 Glue on decorations of your choice.

4 Knot the ends of the elastic. Staple them to the back of the mask.

Imagine That!

Clowns have all different faces and costumes. Decide what type of clown you want to be and create a face that fits. What else can you add to the mask to make your clown character come "alive"? Use your imagination and "try on" a different face. Anything goes!

BiG BeaK

Hey, yellow bird,
with the great big beak,
What kind of worm
do you seek?

What You Need

Large paper plate

Child safety scissors

Stapler

Tempera paints

Paintbrushes

Elastic

◎ More Paper Plate Fun! ◎

Pretend Play: Add some feathers. Put on a cape and a funny hat and become "Super Chicken!"

Story Corner: Read *Poppy & Ella: Three Stories About Two Friends* by Jef Kaminsky and *Henny-Penny* by Jane Wattenberg.

☆ Here We Go! ☆

1 Curl and staple the plate to form a cone.

2 Cut a gap in the top of the cone as shown.

3 Fold up the eye area. Cut out the eye holes.

4 Paint around the eyes and beak.

5 Knot the ends of the elastic; staple them to the back of the mask.

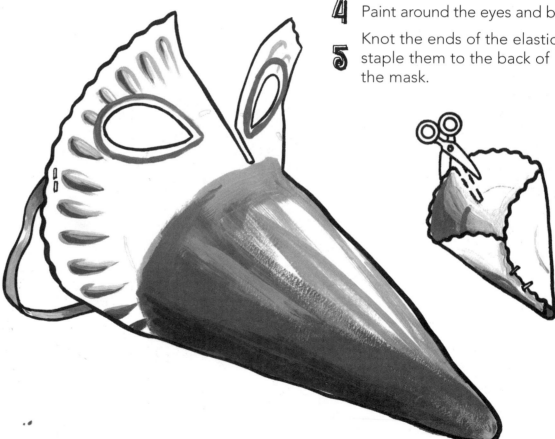

WiSE OLD OWL

Wise old owl comes out at night, Hunting for prey in the moonlight!

40

Imagine That!

Believe it or not, an owl can turn its head almost all the way around and upside down! How far can you turn your head? Make your mask and see just how owl-like you feel then. Who-o-o-o-o-o!

What You Need ✏

Large heavy-duty paper plate

Child safety scissors

Felt

Glue

Large regular paper plate or scraps

Tempera paints

Paintbrushes

Craft feathers

Elastic

Stapler

☆ Here We Go! ☆

1 Cut the paper plate to fit over your mouth and nose. Trim around the top of the plate as shown.

2 Glue on felt to cover the mask. Trim to fit. Cut out the eye holes.

3 Cut two circles, each about $2\frac{1}{2}$" (6 cm) wide, two small triangle-shaped ears, and a triangle-shaped beak from the second plate or scraps. Cut out the center of both circles, making donut-shaped eyes. Paint the eyes, ears, and beak.

4 Glue feathers next to the eye holes. Glue the donut-shaped eyes over the paper-plate eye holes and the ends of the feathers. Staple the ears to the head. Glue on the beak.

5 Knot the ends of the elastic; staple them to the back of the mask.

beak

⊙ More Paper Plate Fun! ⊙

Art Play: Add glasses to make your owl look really wise!

Just for Fun: What letter of the alphabet does an owl's eye look like? How many words can you think of that begin with that letter?

Story Corner: Read *Owl Moon* by Jane Yolen or the famous poem *The Owl and the Pussycat* by Edward Lear. Then, act out the story!

TERRIFIC TIGER

Black and yellow stripes everywhere; The tiger is sunning and hasn't a care!

Imagine That!

Did you know that baby tigers can be called *ligers* or *tigons*? The name depends on whether their daddy was a lion or a tiger. So, what will it be — a baby tiger or a great big daddy cat? You decide!

What You Need

Large paper plate

Child safety scissors

Stapler

Orange and black tempera paints

Paintbrushes

Black pipe cleaner

Elastic

☆ Here We Go! ☆

1 Cut out the paper plate to fit above your mouth and nose.

2 From the scrap, cut out two triangle-shaped ears. Staple them to the paper plate. Cut out the eye holes.

3 Paint your tiger face orange and let dry. Then, paint on some black stripes.

4 Cut a pipe cleaner into two pieces and poke both pieces through the mask for whiskers.

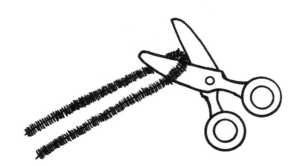

5 Knot the ends of the elastic. Staple them to the back of your mask. Now you're ready for the jungle!

⟳ More Paper Plate Fun! ⟳

Just for Fun: Make a tiger costume. Paint orange stripes on a black sweatshirt and pants. Then, visit a zoo to see a real tiger!

Story Corner: For more tiger fun, read *The Cinder-eyed Cats* by Eric Rohmann.

back view

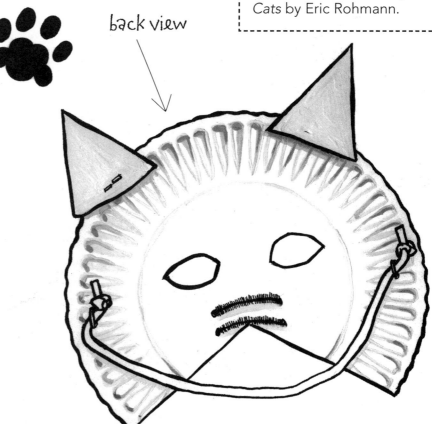

SPACEY SPACEMAN

*Googly-eyed spaceman,
sparkling green;
How many planets
have you seen?*

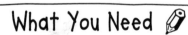
What You Need ✏

Large paper plate

Aluminum foil

Child safety scissors

Egg carton

Glue

Pipe cleaners

Elastic

Stapler

1 Cover the plate with aluminum foil.

2 Cut out eye holes through the plate and the foil.

3 Cover two or more egg-carton sections in foil. Poke eye holes in them and glue them onto the face.

4 Bend one pipe cleaner into an accordion shape and poke it into the plate for the mouth.

5 Poke a spiral-shaped pipe cleaner into the top of the mask (twist to hold) for an antenna.

6 Knot the ends of the elastic; staple them to the back of the mask.

☺ More Paper Plate Fun! ☺

Pretend Play: Get a silver trash bag and *with grown-up help*, make a complete space-man costume! (Remember please: *Never put a plastic bag over your head.*)

HaTs FoR PlaY!

Why does a construction worker wear one kind of hat and a farmer wear another kind? With a little cutting, stapling, and some glue, there's no job you can't do — with just the right hat to keep the sun out of your eyes, the water off your head, and flying objects safely away from you! Pick a hat for work or play; make a new one every day!

ASTRONAUT'S HELMET

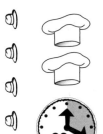

You need this helmet to cover your face. It gives you oxygen when you're up in space!

⊙ More Paper Plate Fun! ⊙

Art Play: For a real spacey helmet, cover your plates with aluminum foil. Turn an appliance-sized cardboard box into your own spaceship!

What You Need ✏

5 large heavy-duty paper plates

Markers or tempera paints and paintbrushes

Stickers and other decorations

Child safety scissors

Stapler

☆ Here We Go! ☆

1 Decorate the plates.

2 Cut out a rectangle at eye level in one plate to use as the front of your helmet.

3 Staple the top plate to the front plate. Then, staple the remaining plates to form your helmet. Get ready for takeoff!

ROBIN HOOD Hat

*Robin Hood —
all dressed in green,
Had many disguises
so he wouldn't be seen!*

What You Need

Large paper plate

Stapler

Elastic

Glue

Feather

Green tempera paint

Paintbrush

⊚ More Paper Plate Fun! ⊚

Just for Fun: Read *The Adventures of Robin Hood* by Marcia Williams.

Put on a Play: Replace the feather with a streamer for a Maid Marian hat. Make hats for Little John, Friar Tuck, and the sheriff of Nottingham.

☆ Here We Go! ☆

1. Curl the plate to form a cone. Staple the rims together where they touch. Turn the front rim up.

2. Knot the ends of the elastic and staple them to the hat.

3. Glue a feather in the top. Paint the hat green and let dry. This hat is made to be worn toward the back of the head.

BaKeR'S Hat

25

*A baker's hat
is tall and white,
With a fluffy top,
it fits just right!*

What You Need ✏️

4 large paper plates

Child safety scissors

Stapler

Tape

White tissue paper

Glue

☆ Here We Go! ☆

1 Cut the bottom rim from three of the plates so that the edges are straight.

2 Staple the three trimmed plates to fit around your head. Put tape over any staples that might pull your hair.

3 Fold the rim of the fourth plate down. Cover it loosely with tissue paper.

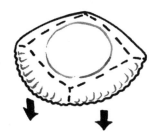

4 Glue the tissue-covered plate on top of the three stapled plates. Since a baker's hat is usually white, there's no need to paint it unless you want to!

cover plate loosely with tissue paper →

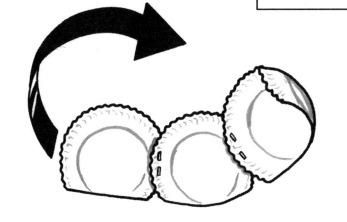

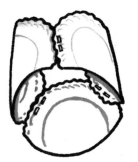

Imagine That!

The tall design of this hat helps a baker's head stay cool while working around a hot oven. What other hat designs help to keep your head cool?

◎ More Paper Plate Fun! ◎

Story Corner: Take a look at the bakers' hats in *Cook-a-Doodle-Doo* by Janet Stevens and Susan Stevens Crummel, and *In the Night Kitchen* by Maurice Sendak. There's even a yummy recipe at the end you might want to try!

CONSTRUCTION WORKER

A construction worker builds roofs and walls. His hard hat protects him from things that fall!

25

Imagine That!

Why do you think construction workers' hats are so brightly colored?

What You Need ✏️

2 large heavy-duty paper plates

(For a BIGGER hat, use $10\frac{5}{8}$" (27 cm) paper plates.)

Child safety scissors

Stapler

Pencil

Yellow tempera paint

Paintbrush

Tape

☆ Here We Go! ☆

1 Cut out four triangles from one plate as shown. Overlap the cut ends and staple together to make a hat.

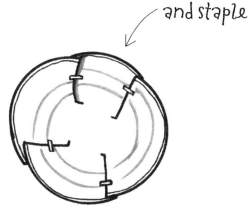

overlap and staple

2 Trace the hat onto the second plate. Cut out the center about 1" (2.5 cm) in from the tracing line.

3 Trim the rim of the second plate to fit the shape of a construction hat. (Don't forget the front brim!) Staple the rim to the top.

4 Lightly paint the hat. Put tape over any staples that might pull your hair. Now you're ready for work!

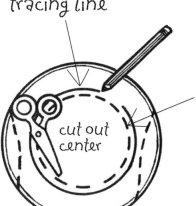

tracing line

cut line

cut out center

trim

◎ More Paper Plate Fun! ◎

Just for Fun: With a grown-up's help, practice using a real hammer by pounding some nails into a piece of wood. Visit a real construction site.

Art Play: Make a tool belt (follow the instructions for the purse or pouch, page 122). Put on your belt and hat, gather some play tools, and get ready to build!

Story Corner: To make fire engines, police cars, cranes, and 'dozers, read *Vroom! Vroom! Making 'dozers, 'copters, trucks & more* by Judy Press.

BUSY FARMER

*The farmer works hard
outside all day,
Tending crops
and stacking hay!*

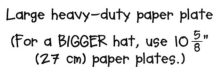

What You Need ✏️

Large heavy-duty paper plate

(For a BIGGER hat, use $10\frac{5}{8}$"
(27 cm) paper plates.)

Child safety scissors

Stapler

Large regular paper plate

Pencil

Tape

Brown or yellow tempera paints

Paintbrushes

☆ Here We Go! ☆

1 Cut out four triangles from the heavy-duty plate. Overlap the cut ends and staple together to make a hat.

2 Trace the hat onto the regular plate. Cut out the center about 1" (2.5 cm) in from the tracing line. Fray the edges of the rim.

3 Staple the top of the hat to the frayed rim. Put tape over any staples that might pull your hair.

4 Lightly paint your hat. Now give it a try!

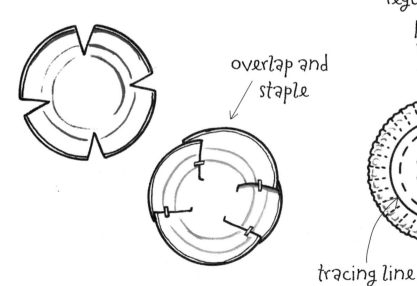

overlap and staple

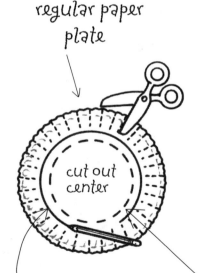

regular paper plate

cut out center

tracing line

cut line

Imagine That!

Why do you think a farmer needs to wear a hat with a wide brim? What else would you wear to dress like a farmer for work in the fields and barns?

⊙ More Paper Plate Fun! ⊙

Art Play: Attach elastic for a chin strap.

Just for Fun: Grow some salad sprouts. Dampen alfalfa, mung bean, or sunflower seeds in a glass jar. Watch how fast the sprouts grow. Now, eat them on a salad!

Story Corner: Read *Who Took the Farmer's Hat?* by Joan L. Nodset.

POLICE OFFICER

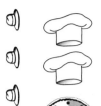

25

No cutting needed!

*A police officer works
the whole day long,
To help us all
when things go wrong!*

POLICE

What You Need 🖉

2 large paper plates

(For a BIGGER hat, use $10\frac{5}{8}$"
(27 cm) paper plates.)

Stapler

Tape

Glue

Tempera paints

Paintbrushes

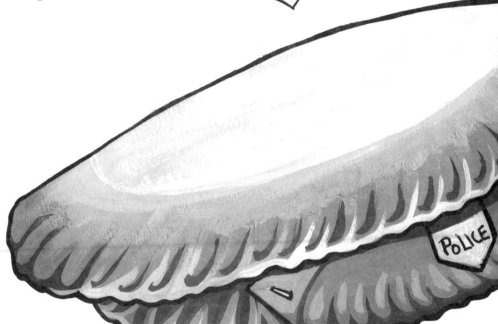

☆ Here We Go! ☆

1 Fold one plate in at the sides and across the front.

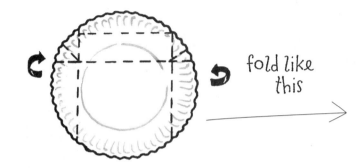

fold like this

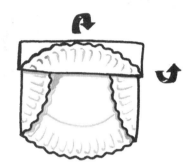

Imagine That!

The police officer's hat has a police *insignia*, or symbol, on it. Design your own insignia with a symbol that will make you feel like a good police officer. What other things are on a police uniform?

2 Tuck the two front corners inside and staple them to hold. Put tape over any staples that might pull your hair.

3 Fold the front rim out for the visor.

fold rim out for visor

4 Glue the second plate on top. Lightly paint the hat a dark color. When the paint is dry, add the police insignia. Are you ready to help people?

glue second plate on top

◎ **More Paper Plate Fun!** ◎

Art Play: Make a gold-painted police badge to go with your hat. Add elastic to hold the hat onto your head while playing.

FiRe FiGHTeR

The fire fighter's hat
protects from harm.
Toss it up on your head
when you hear the alarm!

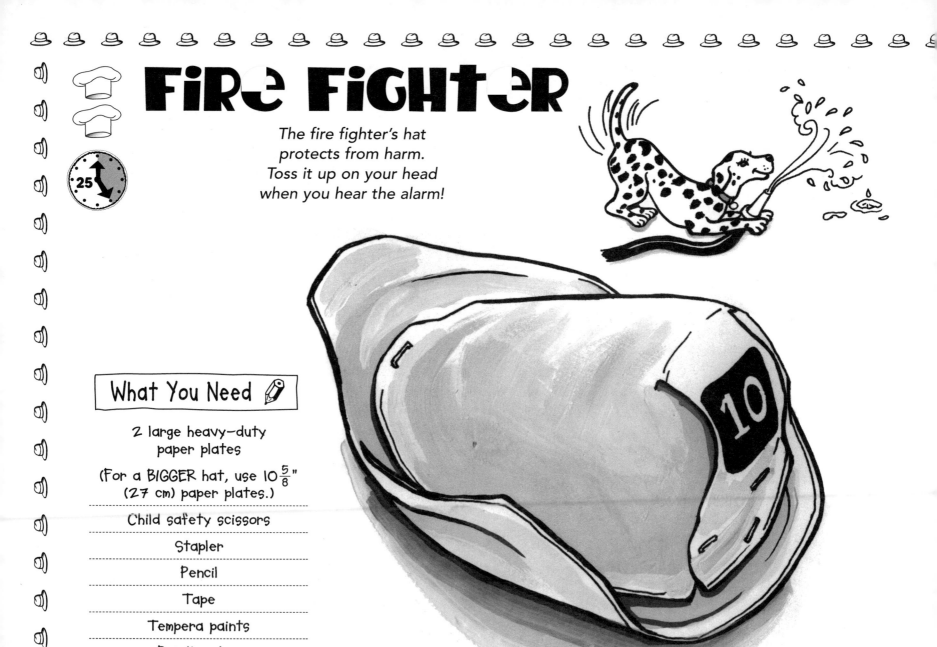

What You Need ✏️

2 large heavy–duty
paper plates

(For a BIGGER hat, use $10\frac{5}{8}$"
(27 cm) paper plates.)

Child safety scissors

Stapler

Pencil

Tape

Tempera paints

Paintbrushes

☆ Here We Go! ☆

1 Make two cuts in one plate as shown. Tuck the cut ends behind the front flap. Staple.

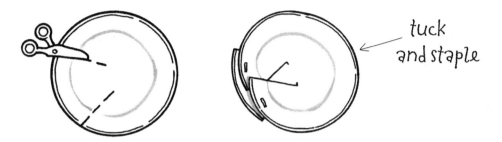

tuck and staple

2 Trace the hat onto the second plate. Cut out the center about 1" (2.5 cm) in from the tracing line.

tracing line

cut line

trim to make a "V"

3 Draw and trim the rim and sides of the second plate to make a "V" at the back.

4 Staple the two plates together to form the hat. Put tape over any staples that might pull your hair. Curl up the side and front rims.

5 Lightly paint your hat. Put your special number on the front!

Imagine That!

A fire fighter's hat is slanted down the back. Can you guess why? That's right; it's designed to let water drain off the fire fighter's head! Every hat also has a special number on it for identification. Choose your favorite number to put on your hat. Then, go over each family member's role in case there's ever a real fire!

☺ More Paper Plate Fun! ☺

Just for Fun: Visit a fire station. Take a tour of the fire trucks and find out what you should do if you're ever in a burning building or car. What number do you dial to call the fire department?

COWBOY Hat

*The cowboy wears
his hat all day
While herding the cattle
so they won't stray!*

What You Need ✏️

2 large paper plates

(For a BIGGER hat, use $10\frac{5}{8}$"
(27 cm) paper plates.)

Child safety scissors

Stapler

Pencil

Tape

Tempera paints

Paintbrushes

String

◎ More Paper Plate Fun! ◎

Art Play: Staple cord or string inside the hat to hold it on when you wear it. Add more string to the hat as decoration. Picture a cowboy in your mind, and make yourself a cowboy vest out of a big paper bag to match your hat.

Story Corner: For stories about cowboys and cowgirls, read *Yipee-Yah: A Book About Cowboys and Cowgirls* by Gail Gibbons and *Sam's Wild West Show* by Nancy Antle.

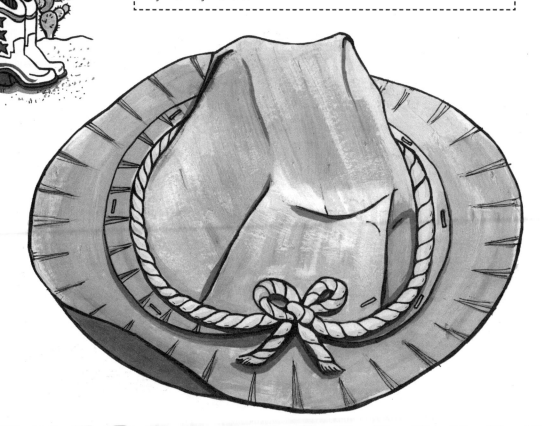

☆ Here We Go! ☆

1 Make four cuts in one plate, two in front and two in back as shown.

2 Gently fold the plate down the middle to make a crease in the top; then, fold down the sides and the front and back flaps.

3 Tuck the cut edges behind the front and back flaps. Staple.

4 Trace the top plate onto the second plate. Cut out the center about $\frac{1}{2}$" (1 cm) in from the tracing line.

5 Lightly press the top plate to the bottom plate and staple them together. Put tape over any staples that might pull your hair. Turn up the bottom rim.

6 Lightly paint your hat. You're ready for the roundup!

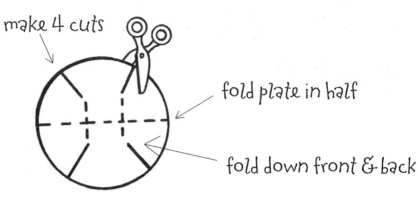

make 4 cuts

fold plate in half

fold down front & back

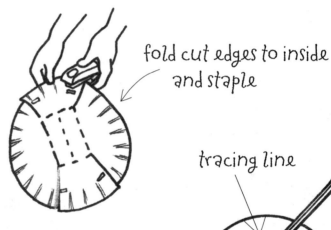

fold cut edges to inside and staple

tracing line

cut line

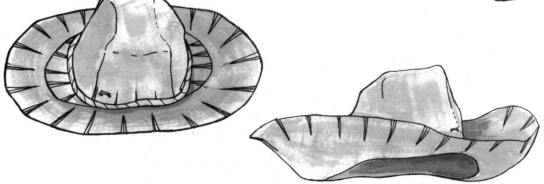

PERFECT PARTY HAT

Decorate a party hat
for your special day;
Invite your friends and family
to eat some cake and play!

What You Need ✏

Large paper plate

Stapler

Child safety scissors

Elastic

Markers or tempera paint
and paintbrushes

Stickers and other decorations

☆ Here We Go! ☆

1 Curl the plate to form a cone. Staple together.

2 Cut the bottom edge so the hat sits level on top of your head.

3 Knot the ends of the elastic and staple them to the hat.

4 Decorate with markers and stickers for ready-to-wear hats, or lightly paint and glue on pom-poms, sequins, and feathers!

curl and staple

Imagine That!

Hats are worn for many different reasons — some for safety, some for style — but this hat is just for fun! Think of all the colors you can mix. Maybe you want a wild pattern, squiggly paper flowers, or a favorite picture pasted on. Your party hat can be any design that will put you in a party mood! Have a good time!

◎ More Paper Plate Fun! ◎

Art Play: For birthday parties at home or school, set up a craft table and let your friends make and decorate their own hats!

Story Corner: Take a look at the party hats in *Spot's Birthday* Party by Eric Hill. Plan a special party for you and your friends with hats, fun food, and games in *Great Parties for Kids* by Nancy Fyke, Lynn Nejam, and Vicki Overstreet.

BASEBALL CAP

*This baseball cap
keeps the sun from your eyes,
So when you're in the outfield
you can catch the pop flies!*

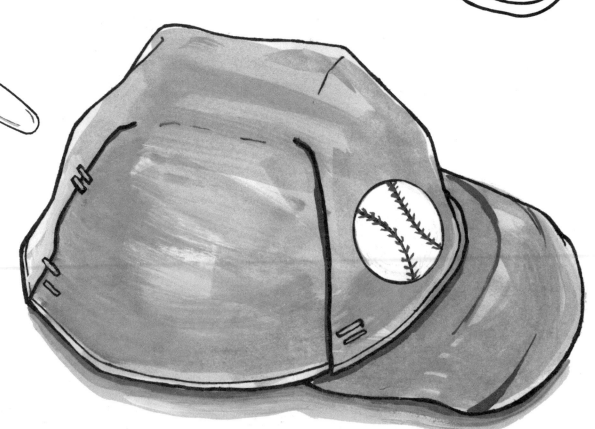

What You Need

2 large heavy-duty
paper plates

(For a BIGGER hat, use $10\frac{5}{8}$"
(27 cm) paper plates.)

Child safety scissors

Stapler

Tape

Tempera paints

Paintbrushes

☆ Here We Go! ☆

1 Cut out four triangles from one plate as shown. Overlap the cut edges and staple together to make a hat.

2 Cut a piece from the second paper plate for the cap's bill. Staple on. Put tape over any staples that might pull your hair.

3 Lightly paint your cap your favorite colors. Then, play ball!

Imagine That!

If you have a favorite baseball or soccer team, make your cap with your team colors. Otherwise, make up your own "home" team colors for your cap!

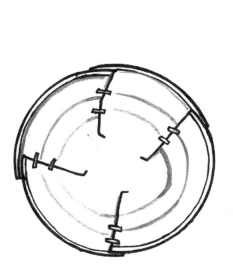

◎ More Paper Plate Fun! ◎

Just for Fun: Decorate your hat with your initials or a favorite sticker. Go to a real ball park to feel what it's like to be part of the crowd!

Art Play: To help keep your hat on better, attach an elastic band to go under your chin. Tie knots in each end of the elastic and staple them to the inside of the cap.

Story Corner: Read about a good way to get ready to play ball in *Max* by Rachel Isadora.

Sun Hat

*Wear a hat
when you're in the sun,
'Cause getting a sunburn
is no fun!*

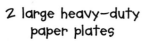

What You Need ✏️

2 large heavy–duty
paper plates

(For a BIGGER hat, use $10\frac{5}{8}$"
(27 cm) paper plates.)

Child safety scissors

Pencil

Stapler

Elastic

Tape

Tempera paints

Paintbrushes

☆ **Here We Go!** ☆

1 Cut out four triangles from one plate as shown. Overlap the cut edges and staple together to form a hat.

 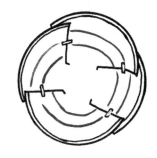

2 Trace the hat onto the second paper. Cut out the center about $\frac{1}{2}$" (1 cm) in from the tracing line. Staple the top and bottom plates together.

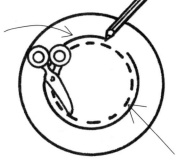

tracing line

cut line

3 Knot the ends of the elastic and staple them to the hat for a chinstrap. Put tape over any staples that might pull your hair.

4 Lightly paint to decorate the hat.

◎ More Paper Plate Fun! ◎

Just for Fun: Try these cool ideas for a sunny day:

(1) Pour fruit juice in an ice-cube tray, place a toothpick in each cube, and freeze for your own **homemade Popsicles!**

(2) **Squeeze some fresh lemons** and have a lemonade stand (but don't forget to wear a hat!).

(3) **Make a sand-castle city** in the sandbox, and then run through the sprinkler to wash off!

Story Corner: For lots of fun in the sun, read *Summer Fun! 60 Activities for a Kid-Perfect Summer* by Susan Williamson.

EGYPTIAN HEAD CREST, COLLAR, AND BELT

Making costumes is such fun; Pretend to be — anyone!

55

Belt

Head Crest

Collar

What You Need ✏️

3 large paper plates

Child safety scissors

Elastic

Decorations

☆ Here We Go! ☆

FOR THE COLLAR:

1 Cut a neck hole in the plate as shown on page 88. Leave a $\frac{1}{4}$" (5 mm) opening so it's easy to put on and take off.

2 Decorate with glitter.

FOR THE HEAD CREST:

1 Cut one paper plate in half. Cut two slits in the plate as shown.

2 Poke a hole about $\frac{1}{2}$" (1 cm) in from each cut. Insert elastic through the holes, and tie or staple it to fit your head.

3 Decorate with glitter.

FOR THE BELT:

1 Cut the leftover unused half of the paper plate in half.

2 Poke two holes in the center of the triangle, $1\frac{1}{2}$" (3.5 cm) apart as shown. Thread elastic through the holes, and staple the ends together so it fits around your waist.

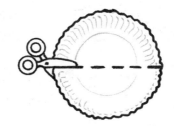

Imagine That!

Make believe you've gone back in time to one of the most amazing civilizations that ever lived! In addition to richly decorated clothing, ancient Egypt is famous for its pyramids. Brainstorm with some friends about building a pretend pyramid.

◎ More Paper Plate Fun! ◎

Story Corner: For some exciting information about ancient Egypt, read *Cleopatra* by Diane Stanley or *Bill and Pete Go Down the Nile* by Tomie dePaola. To learn more about this amazing ancient civilization and make pyramids, read *Pyramids! 50 Hands-On Activities to Experience Ancient Egypt* by Avery Hart and Paul Mantell.

seasonal FUN!

Celebrate the excitement and wonder of the changing seasons — spring, summer, fall, and winter. Do opposites: Make snowflakes in summer, a beach scene in winter, and a bright cheery sun on a cloudy day. When you're playing with paper plates, it doesn't matter what time of year it is or what the weather is like outside — you can create anything you want to!

SUNNY SUNSHINE

*Sunny sunshine
with rays so bright,
Stretching and reaching
way out of sight!*

25

Imagine That!

The sun makes just about everyone feel good. Give your sun a happy expression and lots of glowing rays!

What You Need ✏

2 large paper plates
- - - - - - - - - - - - - - - - - - - -
Child safety scissors
- - - - - - - - - - - - - - - - - - - -
Glue or stapler
- - - - - - - - - - - - - - - - - - - -
Tempera paints
- - - - - - - - - - - - - - - - - - - -
Paintbrushes

☆ Here We Go! ☆

1 Cut out the sun's rays from one plate.

2 Glue or staple the rays to the other plate.

3 Paint the sun and the rays in glorious colors!

◎ More Paper Plate Fun! ◎

Story Corner: Read *When the Sun Rose* by Barbara Helen Berger and *Small Cloud* by Arian.

NORTH STAR

This bright star shines in the night, It sits in the North — oh, what a sight!

15

⊚ More Paper Plate Fun! ⊚

Story Corner: Read *Twinkle, Twinkle, Little Star* by Isa Trapani.

☆ Here We Go! ☆

1 Cut four long and four short points from one plate. Staple them to the rim of the other plate.

2 Glue on glitter to make your star shine!

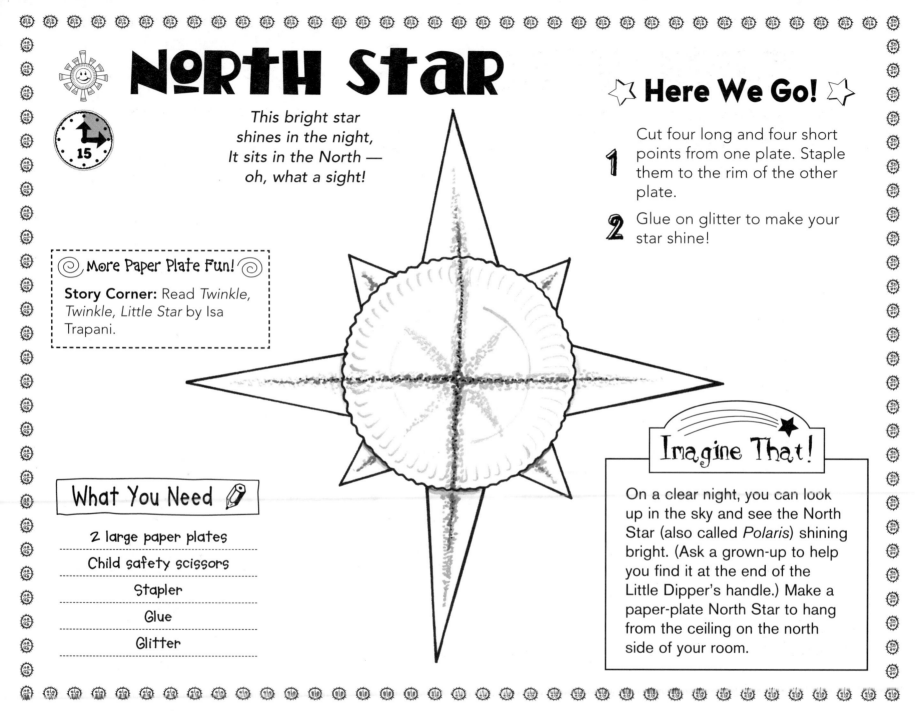

What You Need ✏

2 large paper plates

Child safety scissors

Stapler

Glue

Glitter

Imagine That!

On a clear night, you can look up in the sky and see the North Star (also called *Polaris*) shining bright. (Ask a grown-up to help you find it at the end of the Little Dipper's handle.) Make a paper-plate North Star to hang from the ceiling on the north side of your room.

BALL TOSS TOY

A cup and a ball attached with a string, Get them together with just the right swing!

1 Cut off one-third of the paper plate at the bottom.

2 Staple 12" (30 cm) of string or yarn to the bottom rim of the larger piece.

3 Curl the plate to form a cone and staple it together.

4 Tie the bead onto the end of the yarn.

5 Decorate the cone with stickers.

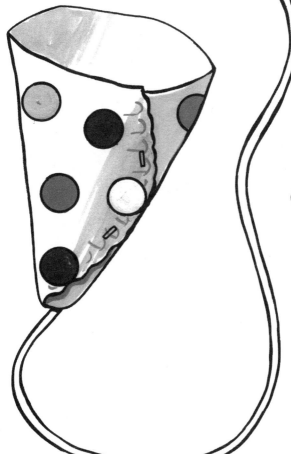

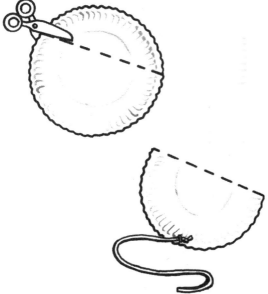

What You Need ✏

Large paper plate

Child safety scissors

Stapler

String or yarn

Large bead

Stickers

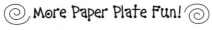

🌀 **More Paper Plate Fun!** 🌀

Art Play: Put another cup at the other end of a longer string, and use it as a telephone with a friend!

PaPer-PLate WiNDSoCK

Do you ever wonder which way the wind blows? Just hang this dandy windsock to be the one who knows!

1 Cut a 3" (7.5 cm) square in the center of the plate.

2 Make four cuts in the plate as shown.

3 Fold the outer sides to the inside, bending the extended edges inward. Staple the flaps to form a rectangle.

4 Decorate with markers, cut-out shapes, or paints. Tape or staple streamers around the bottom rim.

5 Poke holes in the top and tie string or ribbon to hang the windsock. Now watch the streamers blow!

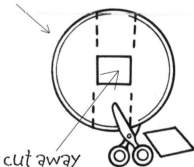

What You Need

Large heavy-duty paper plate

Child safety scissors

Stapler

Markers or tempera paints and paintbrushes

Decorations

Tape

Streamers

Ribbon or string

fold in and staple

bend inward

cut away

SiMPLE SUNDiAL

If you need to know the time, go out in the sun. Put your simple sundial out — it can be lots of fun!

☆ **Here We Go!** ☆

1 Decorate your plate with a sunshine or garden design.

2 Put an "N" near the top of the plate for "north." Above the N, put the number 12. Go around the rim of the plate, marking it like a clock with all the other numbers from 1 to 12.

3 Ask a grown-up to trim the chopstick to about 8" (20 cm) and poke it through the center of the plate. Use glue and tape to hold it in place upright.

4 Take your sundial out on a sunny day. Set the "N" toward the north (ask a grown-up where North is if you're not sure). What time is it?

MOTHER'S DAY BOUQUET

30

*Take a simple plate,
decorated with loving care.
Fill it full of flowers
for a special day to share!*

Imagine That!

How will you celebrate
Mother's Day in your family?
Start with this bouquet or a
bouquet of paper-plate summer
flowers (see page 104). Then,
think of other things to do to
make a day that's extra nice!

What You Need ✏️

2 large paper plates

Child safety scissors

Stapler

Glue

Sponge

Tempera paints

Lace

Marker

Hole punch

Ribbon

Flowers (dried or fresh)

HAPPY MOTHER'S DAY!

☆ Here We Go! ☆

1. Curl one plate into a cone; staple it together.

2. Cut out a heart from the other plate. Glue lace around the heart and print a Mother's Day message on the front.

3. Lightly sponge-paint the outside, inside, and heart. Let everything dry.

4. Glue the heart to the front of the cone.

5. Punch two holes in the top of the paper plate. Tie a ribbon through to hang your gift.

6. Fill the decorated holder with flowers!

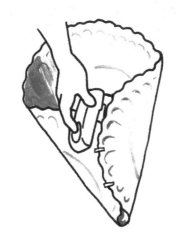

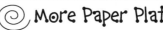

⟳ More Paper Plate Fun! ⟳

Breakfast in Bed: Plan a breakfast in bed for Mom. Make her cinnamon-sugar toast (buttered toast sprinkled with cinnamon and sugar). Decorate a paper place mat and a Mother's Day paper plate to serve the breakfast.

Art Play: For a special design, cut out small leaf or heart shapes from a sponge and lightly sponge the design on. Fill the cone with candies!

Story Corner: Read together *Love You Until* by Lisa McCourt, *Love You Forever* by Sheila McGraw, and *Mothers Are Like That* by Carol Carrick.

SOLAR SYSTEM

*Up in the sky,
way up in the stars,
You can see
Jupiter, Venus, and Mars!*

Imagine That!

Make up a name for a pretend planet and place it where you would imagine it to be in the solar system.

What You Need 🖉

5 large paper plates

Child safety scissors

Pencil

Tempera paints

Paintbrushes

Hole punch

Yarn

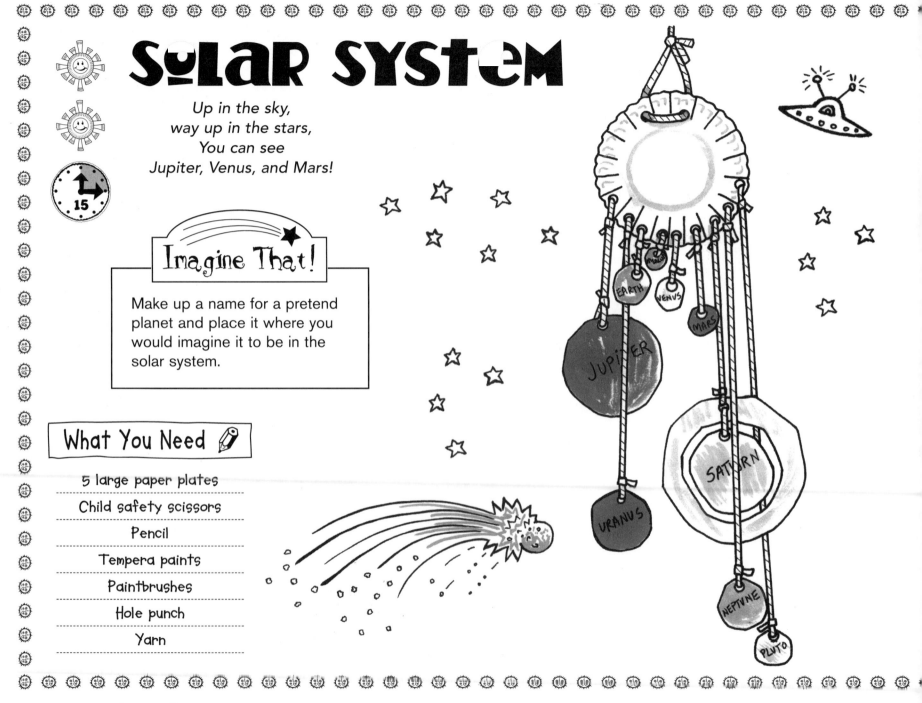

☆ Here We Go! ☆

1 Use one whole plate for the sun. Fray the edges for the sun's rays.

2 Draw and cut out Mercury, Venus, Earth, and Neptune from the second plate. Draw and cut out Pluto, Uranus, and Mars from the third plate. Draw and cut out Jupiter from the fourth plate and Saturn, with its ring, from the fifth plate.

◎ More Paper Plate Fun! ◎

Art Play: Add some asteroids and comets to your solar system.

Story Corner: Discover a lot more about our solar system in *The Golden Book of Stars and Planets* by Judith Herbst.

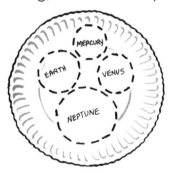

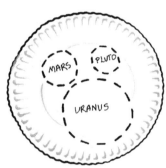

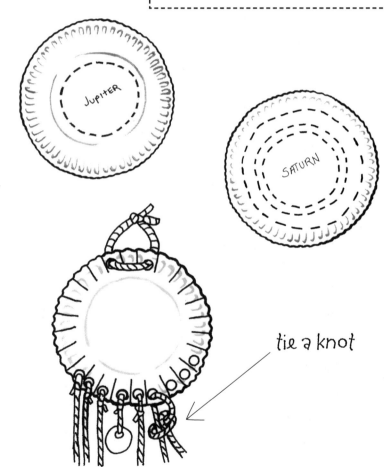

3 Paint all the planets and the sun.

4 Punch a hole in nine of the sun's rays and a hole in each planet. Use yarn to tie the planets onto the sun in the order of how far away from the sun they are.

Start with Mercury, the closest. Hang Venus next, a little lower. Continue with Earth, Mars, Jupiter, Saturn (with the ring), Uranus, Neptune, and Pluto last.

tie a knot

FATHER'S DAY AWARD

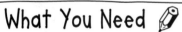

*Make an awesome ribbon
to honor dear ol' Dad,
'Cause he deserves a medal —
it will make him mighty glad!*

ME   DAD

DAD

YOU ARE THE

greatest

What You Need ✏

Large regular paper plate

Child safety scissors

Large heavy–duty paper plate

Stapler

Construction paper

Decorations

Markers or tempera paints
and paintbrushes

☆ Here We Go! ☆

1 Cut a 1" (2.5 cm) rim from the large regular plate.

don't cut all the way through

2 Fray the edges. Staple the frayed rim to the rim of the heavy-duty plate.

3 Cut two 2" x 10" (5 x 25 cm) strips from the construction paper. "Fork" the bottoms, and staple them to the back of the plate.

4 Decorate the award, and write a special title on it with markers or tempera paints.

Imagine That!

What special things do you like to do with your dad, grandfather, a grown-up family friend, or teacher? Make this award to show someone how much you like being together. It's great for Father's Day, but it will make someone feel special any day of the year!

☺ More Paper Plate Fun! ☺

Art Play: Include a homemade gift certificate on the award for a car wash or hugs. Make an award for a friend, neighbor, or family member. Your awards will be extra special because you include your love with them!

Story Corner: Curl up with a special grown-up to read *Daddy is a Doodlebug* by Bruce Degen and *Lots of Dads* by Shelley Rotner and Sheila M. Kelly.

CeLeBRation SHaKeR

Shake your shaker,
make lots of noise;
It's so much fun
to make your own toys!

25

Imagine That!

What else could you put in your shaker to make a different sound? What other instruments could you make with a paper plate? How about a tambourine?

What You Need

Large regular paper plate
Child safety scissors
2 large heavy-duty paper plates
Dry beans or unpopped popcorn
Stapler
Tempera paints
Sponges or paintbrushes

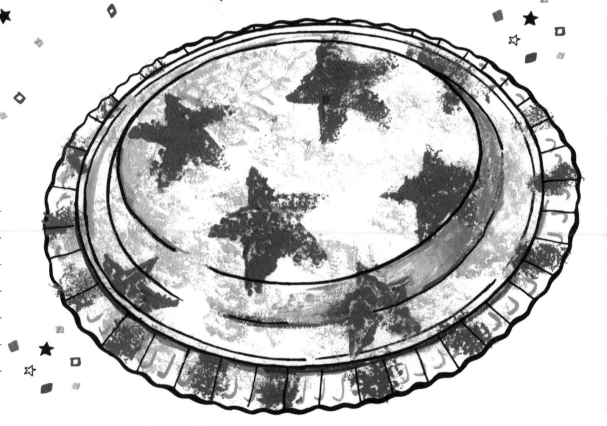

☆ Here We Go! ☆

1 Cut a 1" (2.5 cm) rim from the regular plate. Fray the edges.

2 Put beans or popcorn on one heavy-duty plate. Then, set the frayed rim on top and place the other heavy-duty plate on top of the frayed rim.

3 Staple the heavy-duty plates together, all the way around, with beans inside and the frayed edge sticking out.

4 Paint your shaker.

don't cut all the way through

◎ More Paper Plate Fun! ◎

Art Play: Cut fun shapes like stars, hearts, or moons from a sponge. Lightly dip the shapes into your paints and press them onto your shaker. Or, cut out designs from colored felt and glue them on. Add crepe paper streamers!

Just for Fun: Have a parade with your shakers. Sing and celebrate with lots of noise!

SUMMER FLOWERS

When the frost is gone,
buds begin to show;
And the nice warm sun
causes flowers to grow!

25

What You Need ✏

Large paper plate

Stapler

Child safety scissors

Tempera paints

Paintbrushes or sponges

Pipe cleaners

Glue

Chopstick

Imagine That!

Flowers are all so different!
Some are shaped like bells,
some like circles. Some are
bright colors, some are pure
white. Make your own flowers
to welcome summer, any
color and shape you like!

DRIED FLOWER POUCH

Take two plates,
fill with dried flowers.
Enjoy the bright colors
during winter snow showers!

⭐ Here We Go! ⭐

1 Cut the same size V-shape from both plates.

2 Staple the plates together around the rim.

3 Punch a hole in each top corner.

4 Paint a design with tempera paint.

5 String your ribbon through the holes to hang the pouch. Then, arrange your dried flowers inside.

What You Need ✏️

2 large heavy-duty paper plates

Child safety scissors

Stapler

Hole punch

Tempera paints

Paintbrushes

Ribbon

Dried flowers

🌀 More Paper Plate Fun! 🌀

Just for Fun: Glue three pouches together to file your important mail and artwork! Make a special pouch for someone and give it as a gift.

Story Corner: Read *The Tiny Seed* by Eric Carle and *Round the Garden* by Omri Glaser.

SPARKLING SNOWFLAKE

No matter how far you search,
even up the highest peak,
You'll never find the same snowflakes,
'cause each one is unique!

What You Need ✏️

Large paper plate
- - - - - - - - - - - - - - - - - - - -
Child safety scissors
- - - - - - - - - - - - - - - - - - - -
Glue
- - - - - - - - - - - - - - - - - - - -
Glitter
- - - - - - - - - - - - - - - - - - - -

☺ More Paper Plate Fun! ☺

Story Corner: For some wonderful books about snowflakes, read *Snowflake Bentley* by Jacqueline Briggs Martin, *The Snowy Day* by Ezra Jack Keats, and *White Snow Bright Snow* by Alvin Tresselt.

☆ Here We Go! ☆

1 Fold your plate in half at least three times.

2 Cut out designs from the *folded* edges.

3 Unfold the plate and you have your very own snowflake!

4 Decorate it to make it sparkle.

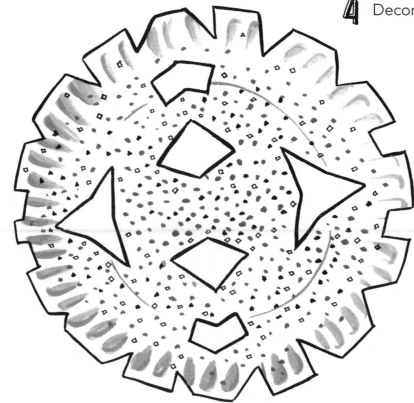

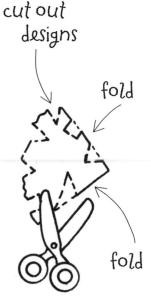

cut out designs

fold

fold

ALL ABOUT ME!

Here's a chapter just for you, to celebrate the things you do! Make a special pocket for your treasures and a picture frame with your great big smile. Or learn to sew with a homemade button and tell time with your very own clock. Don't wait — express it all on a paper plate!

PICTURE FRAME

Tissue paper and glue,
some ribbons or lace,
Add stones, shells, or jewels
and your smiling face!

What You Need ✏️

Large heavy-duty paper plate
- -
Child safety scissors
- -
Tissue paper, markers, or paints
and paintbrushes
- -
Decorations (beads, lace,
buttons, or shells)
- -
Glue and stapler
- -
Tape
- -
Photo (one of you!)
- -
Hole punch
- -
Ribbon

◎ More Paper Plate Fun! ◎

Art Play: Cut two, three, or
four holes in a plate for
smaller photos.

☆ Here We Go! ☆

1 Cut a shape out of the center of
your plate to fit a photo of your
choice.

2 Decorate the plate.

3 Tape a picture to the back of
the frame.

4 Punch two holes in the top. Tie
a ribbon on and hang your
frame up.

I can sew!

*Up through one hole,
down through another,
Practice some more
and surprise your mother!*

What You Need 🖊

Large heavy-duty paper plate

Child safety scissors

Tempera paint

Paintbrush

Yarn

Tape

⊙ More Paper Plate Fun! ⊙

Just for Fun: Start a button collection! Collect all different kinds of buttons, or make your own buttons from clay. Sort your buttons by color or by size.

☆ Here We Go! ☆

1 Cut four holes in the center of the plate.

2 Paint or add a design to your "button."

3 Tape a piece of yarn to the back of the plate. String the yarn through each hole, crisscrossing it in front to make an "X" shape. Repeat several times. Wow! You're sewing!

GOOD SPORT AWARD

*Give an award
(why not today?)
To a friend or a neighbor
who likes to play!*

What You Need

Large heavy-duty paper plate

Tempera paints

Paintbrushes

Markers

Child safety scissors

Construction paper

Stapler

1 Decorate the plate.

2 Cut out two strips from the construction paper. "Fork" the bottoms and staple them to the back of your plate.

3 Decorate the award and write a special saying on it.

⊙ More Paper Plate Fun! ⊙

Art Play: Add a picture of the special person to the award, or congratulate someone who did something nice by making a hero award!

Story Corner: For good books about heroes and friendship, read *Horace and Morris but Mostly Dolores* by James Howe and *Hooway for Wodney Wat* by Helen Lester. Play with your friends with *The Little Hands Playtime! Book* by Regina Curtis.

BiRTHDAY CROWN

*Today's my birthday —
what a special day!
With my friends and family
We'll laugh, sing, and play!*

1 Cut out 3 strips from the plates. Cut a wavy top on each one. Staple them together to fit your head.

2 From the plate scraps, cut out candle shapes, as many as your age! Glue these to the crown.

3 Paint the crown and decorate it!

What You Need 🖉

2 large paper plates

Child safety scissors

Stapler

Glue

Tempera paints

Paintbrushes or sponges

Markers

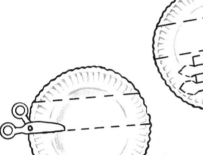

◎ More Paper Plate Fun! ◎

Art Play: Put your name on the crown. Have everyone else at your party make hats to wear, too!

Just for Fun: Host an *unbirthday* party with cake and ice cream and party games but no presents — just to celebrate being with friends.

I'M TELLING TIME!

*Tick, tock,
tick, tock,
Now it's time
to make your clock!*

What You Need ✏

Large paper plate

Markers or tempera paints
and paintbrushes

Child safety scissors

Construction paper or
plate scraps

Paper fastener

☆ **Here We Go!** ☆

1 Paint or draw numbers around the inside rim of your plate, starting with number 12 at the top (ask a grown-up to help with this if needed). Decorate the clock's face.

2 Cut out clock hands from the construction paper. Attach them to the center of the plate with a paper fastener. What time is it on your clock?

Imagine That!

Tick, tock! The seconds, minutes, and hours tick by on the clock! Clocks can be decorated with flowers, cartoon characters, sports equipment, musical notes — whatever you want to see when you look at your clock.

◎ More Paper Plate Fun! ◎

Story Corner: Read *Telling Time with Big Momma Cat* by Dan Harper and *Big Hand, Little Hand: Learn to Tell Time!* by Judith Herbst.

MY SPECIAL THINGS

Fold a little pocket,
hang it on your wall,
Fill it full of special things
or anything at all!

20

No cutting
needed!

What You Need ✏

Large paper plate

Stapler

Markers or tempera paints
and paintbrushes

Decorations

Hole punch

Ribbon

Imagine That!

Do you have special treasures?
The little ones can fit in this
hanging pocket that you can
hang on your closet door or
beside your bed.

☆ Here We Go! ☆

◎ More Paper Plate Fun! ◎

Just for Fun: Use your pocket to save a special collection of coins, erasers, shells, or cards. Or, put some dried flowers in it and give it as a gift!

1 Fold the sides of your plate in. Then, fold the bottom up, leaving the back side taller than the front.

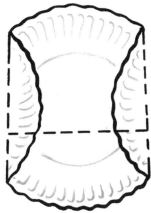

3 Decorate the pocket.

4 Punch one or two holes in the back and tie with ribbon. Now, hang it on your wall!

2 Staple the front to the back.

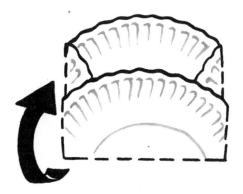

FOOD FRACTIONS

*What kind of food
will decorate your plate?
Cut it up in pieces
until you make it eight!*

What You Need

3 or 4 large paper plates

Tempera paints

Paintbrushes

Felt

Child safety scissors

Glue

☆ Here We Go! ☆

1 Decorate your plates like a favorite food.

2 Cut your plates into pieces — as many as you need. Then, match them up again!

Imagine That!

What kinds of foods do people usually cut up into equal parts? Do you want to create something to share with two or more people?

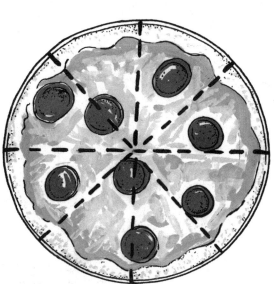

◎ More Paper Plate Fun! ◎

Just for Fun: Make a real pizza or cake with a grown-up and practice your fractions while serving!

Story Corner: Read *Eating Fractions* by Bruce McMillan.

MY VERY OWN PURSE (OR POUCH)

No cutting needed!

*A purse of my own
to carry all day,
Filled with my things
so I can play!*

What You Need

Large paper plate

Stapler

Sponges

Tempera paints

Glue

Decorations (lace, flowers)

Hole punch

Ribbon or yarn

☆ Here We Go! ☆

1 Fold the sides of the plate in toward the center.

2 Fold the plate in half and staple it at the sides.

3 Lightly sponge paint the purse and let it dry.

4 Glue on decorations.

5 Punch two holes in the top at each side, through the front and back. Pull a ribbon or yarn through the holes and tie it in front, leaving plenty to hang on your shoulder.

Imagine That!

What do you like to carry in a pouch? Do you like one that closes tightly, or one that's always open at the top? What will you add to your design to make it just the way you want it?

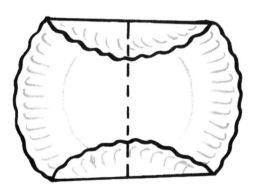 

⊚ More Paper Plate Fun! ⊚

Art Play: Instead of making shoulder straps, punch two holes in the back and wear it on your belt for a handy pouch! Put one together for a carpenter's tool belt! For more construction wear, make the construction hat on page 72.

Story Corner: Read *Lily's Purple Plastic Purse* by Kevin Henkes.

PUZZLE FUN

*Paint a plate
with your own design,
Then cut up the pieces
and see how many you can find!*

1 Paint or draw a picture that covers the whole plate. Let dry.

2 Draw curvy lines on the back of the plate to divide the picture into six or eight pieces.

3 Number each piece, then cut it out.

4 Mix up your pieces and put the design back together again!

What You Need

Large paper plate

Markers or tempera paints

Paintbrushes or sponges

Pencil

Child safety scissors

Imagine That!

Puzzle pieces come in all sizes, shapes, and designs. Paint a picture or cut out a big magazine picture to make a paper-plate puzzle and see if your friends can put it back together.

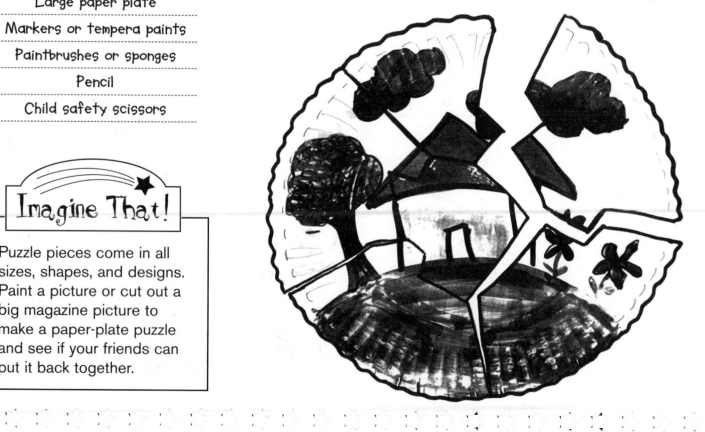

Activity Index by Skill Level

Check the symbol at the beginning of each activity to quickly assess the challenge level.

*Activities with an asterisk involve no cutting.

EASY

MEDIUM

CHALLENGING